William J. Fay

Reading the
Gospel of John

An Introduction

_by_

Kevin Quast

PAULIST PRESS
New York, N.Y./Mahwah, N.J.

Cover art courtesy of The Metropolitan Museum of Art, Gift of J. Pierpont Morgan, 1917 (17.190.38). Copyright © By The Metropolitan Museum of Art.

The Scripture quotations contained herein are from the New Revised Standard Version of the Bible, copyrighted 1989 by the Division of Christian Education of the National Council of the Churches of Christ in the United States of America, and are used by permission. All rights reserved.

Maps by Frank Sabatté, C.S.P.

Copyright © 1991 by
Kevin Quast

Library of Congress Cataloging-in-Publication Data

Quast, Kevin.
    Reading the Gospel of John: an introduction/by Kevin Quast.
      p. cm.
    Includes bibliographical references and index.
    ISBN 0-8091-3297-4 (pbk.)
    1. Bible. N.T. John—Introductions. I. Title.
BS2615.2.Q83 1991
226.5′061—dc20   91-32111
                                                      CIP

Published by Paulist Press
997 Macarthur Boulevard
Mahwah, New Jersey 07430

Printed and bound in the
United States of America

CONTENTS

GUIDE TO CHARTS AND MAPS

Acknowledgments

This book is dedicated to the members of Donway Baptist Church in grateful recognition of their prayers and encouragement.

There are others who deserve thanks. At Ontario Theological Seminary, my students and colleagues perceptively critiqued my thoughts. At his desk, Larry Matthews skillfully edited my manuscript. At home, Sandra, Kira, and Graham exercised supreme patience as I struggled to keep on schedule.

Kevin Quast
June, 1991

Chapter 1

A GOSPEL FOR ALL READERS

Introduction

The pattern is repeated time and time again. The process starts simply enough with a favorite verse or two. It isn't long, however, before readers of the Gospel of John find themselves caught up in the most engaging document in the New Testament. The curious attraction that John has for its readers has several possible explanations.

First, it is a *Gospel for all readers*. At any stage in your Christian journey you can read the Gospel of John with appreciation. New Christians are consistently directed by mature friends to begin their personal Bible reading in John. They soon find themselves carried away in a pristine world of spirituality, truth, and encouragement. Disciples of many years look again and again to its pages for wisdom and insight. Many a sermon has been inspired by the pastor's habitual return to this theological masterpiece. Scholarly attempts to mine the depths of its mysteries continue to multiply down through the centuries.

John has captured the wonderful ability of Jesus to touch the hearts of people throughout their spiritual journey. Jesus meets many different people here in the pages of this Gospel, encountering each one where he or she is at, responding to the level of faith and insight each has.

Second, the appeal of the Fourth Gospel is the appeal of a *Gospel of the symbolic*. The narratives, discourses and interpretations relayed by the evangelist abound with symbolism. A literalistic, superficial reading of John will leave you with an odd sense that you are missing something in the otherwise apparently insignificant descriptive details, numbers, dualisms, ambiguous statements, and peculiar

1

stylistic features. Truth and falsehood, light and darkness, love and hate, above and below: all of these dualisms permeate John so that no incident or statement can be interpreted apart from these categories. Seven signs, seven "I am" sayings, six stone waterpots, three denials and a threefold restoration for Peter, 153 fish; these numbers all have meaning. Jesus uses words with double-meanings to reveal his message to the discerning listener. References to "water," "wine," "bread," "flesh," and "blood" are all ripe with symbolic significance in the Johannine scheme. Even the deliberate and persistent anonymity of the Beloved Disciple itself has a symbolic function. All of the actions and words of Jesus point to something deeper, so the reader is drawn into the mysteries that lie behind the words.

Third, the Gospel is a *Gospel of glory*. Christ is presented in terms of one who is in control from the time of creation through to his passage back to the Father. While on earth, Christ is the glory of God in the flesh. He is a shining light in the darkness. His discourses have the character of revelatory pronouncements. He consciously ushers in his own hour of glorification which culminates in victory on the cross. The Christian reader cannot fail to take heart in him. Hope, optimism, and encouragement well up for readers in a dark, oppressive world as they see the glory of God reflected in the Johannine Jesus.

Fourth, the Gospel is a *Gospel of the Spirit*. In the farewell of Jesus to his disciples we are introduced to a new title for the Holy Spirit: the Paraclete. In the most personal representation of him in the New Testament we discover someone who will be with us, within us, forever. He will remind us of all that Jesus said and did. He will be enabling us to reach out to the world. He will work in the hearts of unbelievers, convincing them of their sinfulness, Christ's righteousness, and ensuing judgment. The Fourth Gospel takes us a step closer than we have ever been before in an understanding of the Third Person of the Trinity. Jesus' direct statements reveal the close relationship between the Spirit, Son and Father.

Fifth, the Gospel is a *Gospel for disciples*. Every Christian, regardless of his or her place in the church today, can read the Gospel of John and find it personally applicable. Instead of elevating a particular group of believers by virtue of their authority or function in the church, John portrays every believer as related to Christ in a similar way. All members of the community of faith are disciples of Jesus. All have equal access to Jesus and his teachings. The call to discipleship in the Gospel transcends time and place.

Sixth, the Gospel is a *Gospel of the present*. John describes the "new age" ushered in by Christ as beginning in the present life of those who accept his claims. Eternal life is lived even now! Those who respond negatively have already entered into judgment. While there is still a hope expressed for a future culmination of God's salvation, John focuses on the quality of the abundant life Christ enables his disciples to live here and now.

For whatever reason you have decided to study the Gospel of John, this book is designed to aid you in your interpretation of what it has to say. As with any New Testament document, we cannot read this Gospel literalistically as if it were a simple narrative of events. Our task is to discover the key that unlocks the cryptic statements of this Gospel. The key to interpreting the Gospel of John can be summarized in one phrase: redemption by relationship. John teaches that salvation comes through believing and knowing the incarnation of faith and truth. Eternal life is lived in relationship to Jesus, God on earth. This relationship involves intimacy, trust, understanding, obedience, and a unity of action and will.

Redemption by relationship is expressed in many ways in the Gospel. It is modeled in the relationships that exist within the Trinity. It is inherent in the sacramental language of the Gospel. It is demonstrated by the prayers, discussions, teachings and actions of Jesus. Even our relationships with one another become part of the experience of eternal life. Life in the community of faith is life in relationship to God and his family. Our final hope is described as the perfection of our relationship with Jesus.

To use our key to unlock the Johannine mysteries, we must first enter into the world of the first century writer and readers. Here we may see how their expression of faith was conditioned by their relationships to Christ, to one another, and to those outside of their tightly knit community.

The Background to the Gospel

Even a superficial reading of the Gospel of John reveals a difference between it and the Synoptics, due to a number of factors, including the cultural milieu at the time and place of writing, the specific nature of the community from which the document arose, and the purpose for writing.

The Jewish Base of the Gospel

Increasingly, scholars are agreeing that the principal background for Johannine thought was the Palestinian Judaism of Jesus' time, although it was in vogue in the 1950s and 1960s to see the Gospel of John as a later Hellenistic work in spite of a remote Jewish connection. The Greek foundation was seen in the use of the concept of the Logos in John 1:1–18, the explanation of Jewish terms for Greek readers, and the presence of certain language and imagery associated with Gnostic traditions.

While the fourth evangelist may have been concerned, in part, to counter attitudes that were giving rise to movements that would lead to Gnosticism, other factors suggest that we should not assume direct Hellenistic sources. In a time when Judaism was gaining many expressions, a number of streams of Jewish belief may have made fundamental contributions to the particular theology of John. For example, the Wisdom tradition likely contributed to the development of the Logos concept. Rabbinic Judaism speaks of God's use of an agent in creation, as does John. John's descriptions of a transcendent Son of Man are close to those of apocalyptic Judaism. There are striking theological and terminological affinities between the Gospel of John and the Dead Sea Scrolls of the Qumran sect. Finally, John shares certain concerns with Samaritan Judaism. The Fourth Gospel, then, has a fundamentally Palestinian Jewish origin, though it is also evident that its final form is directed toward a Greek readership removed from Palestine.

More specifically, the author of the Gospel stamped the Gospel with the marks of his own unique situation and perspective. Who wrote the Gospel? To whom was it written? Fortunately, the Gospel itself gives us some revealing answers to these important questions.

The Beloved Disciple and His Community

The final chapter of the Gospel of John, in referring to the Beloved Disciple, ends with a claim to source and veracity: " . . . This is the disciple who is testifying to these things and has written them; and we know that his testimony is true" (Jn 21:24).

It is clear from this verse that the Beloved Disciple is at least the source behind the Gospel of John. What is not as clear, however, is the identity of the Beloved Disciple. In the patristic writings of the second to the fourth centuries we see how the Beloved Disciple came to be associated with the name John, but if we had only the Gospel itself we might never have made the connection. While his actual role as evangelist requires qualification, a strong case can be made that the Beloved Disciple served as the hero of a particular Christian community, their link to Jesus, and the model of a disciple in close, believing relationship to the Lord.

Recently scholars have focused on identifying and describing the history and characteristics of the Christian community united by their common allegiance to the Beloved Disciple as reflected in the Gospel and epistles of John. A working hypothesis has emerged: the Gospel can be read as a history of a unique community that carried its own sense of identity into the second generation of the Christian church.

From its earliest stage, the Johannine community displayed certain doctrinal and ethical characteristics that served to distinguish them from other Christians. The most obvious distinction of this group was their allegiance to the Beloved Disciple and his witness to Jesus. They held to a uniquely high view of Christ and his preexistence. Their stress on the individual's relationship with God through belief in Jesus overshadowed any development of church structure and pastoral office.

The Johannine Christians were conscious of their differences with other groups, especially in their understanding of Christ. Johannine Christians appealed to the Holy Spirit as the guiding authority in matters of faith, equating the Spirit (Paraclete) with the abiding presence of the ascended Jesus. This spiritual basis for personal authority would prove to be divisive in the group by the time the Johannine epistles were written (note esp. 1 Jn 2:19). As the Johannine churches wrestled with internal divisions, the orthodox eventually merged with the greater Christian church, thereby enriching both traditions as they moved into the second century and on.

As need arises in later chapters we will examine specific matters of background and context. However, it is now important to turn our attention to some literary questions, such as: How does the Fourth Gospel relate to the other three? What was the purpose for writing the Gospel? What process led to the present form of the Gospel? How is it structured?

The Literary Character of the Gospel

Both in content and style, the Gospel of John stands apart from the Synoptics. In content, the differences are striking and easily demonstrated. The Fourth Gospel does not have basic material which the Synoptics record; the Gospel of John presents material integral to its presentation of the life of Christ that is curiously absent in the Synoptic accounts; John includes graphic details in what are otherwise general narratives in the Synoptics; and, more notably, there are apparent discrepancies with the Synoptics in some key aspects of the chronology of Jesus' ministry.

By using the tools of source and redaction criticism, we are able to conclude that the author of the Gospel of John probably was influenced by some of the same traditions that Mark and Luke built upon. In other words, John was not completely independent of Synoptic traditions. Nevertheless, we have to conclude also that John did not come from the same mold as the Synoptics. He has his own independent and early source from which he composed most of his Gospel, offering a largely historical eyewitness account coupled with an independent interpretation of the teachings of Jesus.

Composition and Arrangement

Even apart from its relationship to the Synoptic tradition, the composition of the Gospel of John presents inherent literary inconsistencies which have led scholars to conclude that the Gospel developed progressively over a period of time.

The most plausible reconstruction runs along the following lines: An eyewitness, the Beloved Disciple, stood at the origin of the Gospel tradition, so that the basic Gospel was made up of original and independent oral tradition. The writer of the Gospel, perhaps the Beloved Disciple himself, took these traditions and put them in a fixed, literary form represented by the signs and discourses so characteristic of John. Later, the evangelist or an editor reworked this "first edition," adding some more liturgical and kerygmatic material, such as the prologue, chapter 6 and chapters 15–17. Explanations of Jewish material for a Greek audience may have been made here, as well. Eventually, after the death of the Beloved Disciple, a final editor, in response to felt needs in the community, added chapter 21 and perhaps the account of the woman taken in adultery. There are many finer points to make within these broad strokes, but the result reveals a community production over a period of time. This approach best accounts for the literary evidence while still maintaining the integrity of the Gospel as an independent historical source and theological treatise.

Purpose for Writing

Various stages of writing may mean that there were varied purposes behind the writing of the Gospel. Nevertheless, an original and pervasive purpose gave the Gospel its impetus. The clearest statement of purpose comes right from the Gospel itself: " . . . that you may come to believe that Jesus is the Messiah, the Son of God, and that through believing you may have life in his name" (Jn 20:30–31).

A natural question is, "Was John written for Christians or non-Christians?" If the Johannine community was a group with clear delineations from others, then we should expect the material in the Fourth Gospel to dwell on the need for community members to believe in Jesus completely and to know him intimately. Since true belief and knowledge is an ongoing life commitment, as we shall see in our study, this is an appropriate emphasis for members of the community. In light of this, we should regard the Gospel primarily as an in-house document written for Christian disciples within the Johannine community. It was not designed as an evangelistic tract to outsiders and non-Christians.

Structure

The structure of the Gospel itself makes a distinction between a public and private ministry of Jesus, leading to the conclusion that much of what Jesus says is directed to those who are already part of the community of faith. Chapter 12 of the Gospel ends on the note of Jesus withdrawing from public life, hiding himself from the crowd, no longer performing signs and no longer speaking to them. Chapter 13 begins with the statement that Jesus' hour of glorification has come. He now turns his attention completely to his disciples that he may show them the full extent of his nature and work. The two main sections of the Gospel are appropriately introduced by a prologue and later concluded with a clear epilogue, so the whole Gospel can be seen in one perspective as follows (adapted from Raymond E. Brown, *The Gospel According to John I-XII* [*The Anchor Bible*], vol. 29 [New York: Doubleday, 1966], p. CXXXVIII):

I. *PROLOGUE*
(Jn 1:1–18)

An early hymn which serves as an overture
to the Gospel theme of
"the word becoming flesh."

II.   *THE BOOK OF SIGNS*
                       Public Ministry (Jn 1:19–12:50)

                       Relates Jesus' public ministry of
                       revelation by sign and word.
                       The dilemma of decision is posed to all;
                       some believe but others reject him.
                       His "hour" has not yet come

III.   *THE BOOK OF GLORY*
                       Private Ministry (Jn 13:1–20:31)

                       Jesus' "hour" has come.
                       Turning his attention to his disciples,
                       he reveals his full glory in his hour
                       of return to the Father: the crucifixion.
                       The Spirit is now given to his disciples.

IV.   *EPILOGUE*
                       (Jn 21:1–25)

                       This chapter is added later to the Gospel
                       proper in order to preserve some material
                       and meet new community concerns.

In addition to the over-arching structure of John, we are able to discern sub-structures in the Gospel. These sub-structures are built upon guiding principles and literary features that are, in themselves, keys to interpretation. As we encounter these sub-structures in our study, we will realize that the Gospel of John is a carefully constructed theological presentation, born out of a rich background and an intimate and vital relationship with Christ. Through the community's experiences, the Gospel of John matured to the point that it has become our single richest source of theological reflection on Christ.

STUDY QUESTIONS

1. What attracts you to the Gospel of John?

2. What is the central theme of the Gospel?

3. List at least four streams of Palestinian Judaism that might have

influenced Johannine thought. How do these possible influences affect a theory of direct Greek influence upon the Gospel?

4. How does the Gospel describe its author?

5. What are some of the basic characteristics of the Johannine community?

6. Outline four possible stages in the process of the Gospel's composition.

7. Was John written primarily for Christians or non-Christians?

8. How does the structure of John help answer the above question?

Chapter 2

JESUS CHRIST: GOD IN THE FLESH
(John 1)

Introduction

The small Johannine community obviously stood to benefit from a merger with the greater apostolic stream. However, such a development was also providential for the rest of Christendom: the church inherited what is now her dominant view of Christ. Our belief in Christ as the pre-existent creator who descended from heaven testifies to our acceptance of the Johannine Jesus.

Just as a canyon side reveals different strata of the earth's formation, the Gospel of John displays different christological strata, even within its first chapter. In the prologue (vv. 1–18), we find a unique and highly developed presentation of Jesus as the Logos, the pre-existent rational orderer behind creation who became human so that we might see God. Aspects of Jesus' messianic character are communicated as well in a series of titles in verses 19–51. These titles might be construed as the Beloved Disciple's first impressions of Jesus.

The Logos

Jesus is the Logos, the "Word" of God. He is identified as such in John's prologue (Jn 1:1–18) and nowhere else in the New Testament. Given the most common meaning of the Greek term "logos," its theological significance may be surprising. "Logos," like its English equivalent, refers to anything meaningful. A quick look in the English dictionary under the term "word" will illustrate the wide range of meanings that can also apply to "logos" in Greek. However, in John the word becomes the most notable term of choice to refer to God's self-revelation to humanity, most profoundly and ultimately in Jesus Christ.

In a number of Greek philosophies, the term "logos" was impregnated with significance, which may explain John's choice of this otherwise mundane word. The Stoics, as early as the third century B.C., used it to speak of the cosmic scale of reason which gave the world order, meaning, and congruity. Philo of Alexandria, writing immediately before the New Testament era, was deeply affected by the popular current combination of Stoicism and Platonism. In addition, as a Jew, he turned to the Old Testament for authoritative guidance as he formulated his conceptions of the "logos" as an impersonal means of divine creation and government in the world.

Some of the aspects of the "word" in the Old Testament which impressed Philo were also foundational for the Johannine doctrine of the Logos. Specifically, the word of God was referred to in the context of God's creation of the world. In Genesis 1 we read over and over again " . . . And God said . . . and there was . . ." God created the world by his word. Israel's wisdom schools took this conception of the creative word of God a step further when it identified it with the personification of wisdom. Wisdom became the active agent through which God created the world. Wisdom embodied the word of God (see box). The rabbis subsequently developed this line of thinking to speak of the Torah as the creative word of God (e.g., Gen. Rab. 1).

The presentation of Jesus as the Logos of God in John extends beyond all other similar conceptions, Christian or otherwise, to give us the New Testament's ultimate insight into the divine mind which ordered the world and provides the key to its meaning.

The first obvious teaching of the prologue is that the Logos is pre-existent: he existed before anything was created. The introductory phrase "In the beginning . . . " (Jn 1:1; cf. Gen 1:1) brings the reader to that incomprehensible time when nothing else but God existed. The Logos is so important that he could not simply have come into being like any other person or object.

That the Logos existed before creation does not preclude his relationship to creation. In fact, the Logos was the agent of creation of the world on behalf of God the Father. While "In the beginning" sets the context of the creation account, verse 3 is explicit: "... all things came into being through him, and without him not one thing came into being." Christ, the Word of God, was the hand of God which created the world. The earliest Christians obviously thought that Christ could create new life through redemption, but the idea of

WISDOM PERSONIFIED AND ACTIVE IN CREATION

Compare John's presentation of the Logos to Wisdom personified in Israel's wisdom literature:

The Lord created me at the beginning of his work,
    the first of his acts of long ago.
Ages ago I was set up,
    at the first, before the beginning of the earth.
When there were no depths I was brought forth,
    when there were no springs abounding with water.
Before the mountains had been shaped,
    before the hills, I was brought forth —
when he had not yet made earth and fields
    or the world's first bits of soil.
When he established the heavens, I was there,
    when he drew a circle on the face of the deep,
when he made firm the skies above
    when he established the fountains of the deep,
when he assigned the sea to its limit,
    so that the waters might not transgress his command,
when he marked out the foundations of the earth,
    then I was beside him, like a master worker;
and I was daily his delight,
    rejoicing before him always,
rejoicing in the inhabited world
    and delighting in the human race.

(Proverbs 8:22–31)

O God of my fathers and Lord of mercy,
    who has made all things by thy word,
and by thy wisdom has formed man,
    to have dominion over the creatures thou has made,
and rule the world in holiness and righteousness,
    and pronounce judgment in uprightness of soul,
give me the wisdom that sits by thy throne,
    and do not reject me from among thy servants.

(The Wisdom of Solomon 9:1–4; RSV)

Wisdom will praise herself,
    and glory in the midst of her people.
In the assembly of the Most High she will open her mouth,
    and in the presence of his host she will glory:
"I came forth from the mouth of the Most High,
    and covered the earth like a mist.
I dwelt in high places,
    and my throne was in a pillar of cloud.
Alone I have made the circuit of the vault of heaven
    and have walked in the depths of the abyss.
In the waves of the sea, in the whole earth,
    and in every people and nation I have gotten a possession.
Among all these I have sought a resting place;
    I sought in whose territory I might lodge."

(The Wisdom of Jesus the Son of Sirach 24:1–7; RSV)

creating life is stretched farther back by John to say that this redeeming person is also the agent of divine creation.

The Logos is not an absentee creator. He is also the sustainer and redeemer. "In him was life, and the life was the light of all people" (Jn 1:4). Life and light continue to come to creation through the Logos. In other words, John is claiming that there is no one better to recreate new life and restore our relationships to God, others, and the rest of creation than the person who created it in the first place, the Logos of God.

The Logos is able to offer life because he represents God. The Logos is the fullness of divine revelation. In saying both that the Logos "was with God and was God" (Jn 1:1), the Logos is presented both as related to and identical with God. In as simple and profound a way as possible, absolute unity and diversity are wedded to one another in the nature of God.

Because the Greek does not include an article with the second occurrence of the word "God," this verse has been the subject of perpetual controversy in the debates surrounding the divinity of Jesus. While there are various alternate translations of these phrases, as long as we realize that in some mysterious way there is more to the total being of God than can be expressed in any single member of the Trinity, then the translation "the Word was God" is our most accurate.

To the extent that we understand the Logos, we comprehend what we can of God. The climax of the teaching about the Logos in this hymn is found in verse 14: "And the Word became flesh and lived among us, and we have seen his glory, the glory as of the Father's only Son, full of grace and truth." The Logos became flesh and, as a consequence, humanity was able to see God in the Logos.

The divinity of Christ is boldly affirmed and the human embodiment of God explicitly presented in this passage. These two ideas are bound together to make a powerful statement: the Logos did not merely descend upon or enter into Jesus, the Logos of God became the human nature he bore. The life of Jesus is the history of God himself on earth. Whatever else this teaches, it should serve as a caution against constructing a false dichotomy between what is divine and what is human.

The words "lived among us" in verse 14 are an allusion to the Exodus. They communicate the transient nature of the incarnation and its function as the manifestation of the power and presence of God. The verb translated "lived" means "to pitch a tent," thus implying the temporary nature of the Logos' sojourn on earth. Throughout the Exodus narratives similar language is used to refer to both the tent of meeting and the tabernacle. The reference to seeing the glory of God in John 1:14 further confirms these associations, for just as the glory of God was manifested in the tabernacle (Ex 33:7–11; 40:34–38), so it is revealed in the Logos. God actually came and resided on earth for a time as the Logos, passing through to lead the way in a second Exodus.

In summary, Christ as Logos existed before all time. He created the world. He is God. He temporarily became a human being. These profound truths provide the basis for our understanding of all else. If the Logos became flesh, then to discover the revelation of God, we must begin by turning to Jesus, the complete incarnate Word of God. The Logos is the starting point. In turn, Jesus will shed light on our understanding of the rest of the universe.

The rest of the Gospel presents Jesus as the Logos made flesh. Although the Gospel proper does not use the title Logos of Jesus, it nonetheless depends upon the prologue for the presuppositions with which to read the rest of the Gospel. We see reflected in the prologue the very structure of the Gospel itself. The revelation of the Son, and ensuing rejection by some and acceptance by others is anticipated in the structure of the prologue: revelation (vv. 1–5); rejection (vv. 6–11); acceptance (vv. 12–18).

A Note on Following Jesus

The theme of rejection and acceptance prompts an interruption to the hymn of the prologue. The parenthetical statement (Jn 1:6–8) notes the important testimonial function John the Baptist played in the coming of the Logos. A quick overview of the first chapter of the Gospel further reveals a theme of following Jesus that is related to the testimony of John the Baptist. Combined with other indications such as John 1:15, 3:22–30, 4:1–2 and 5:31–40, the point becomes clear: the Baptist's ministry is singularly important, but it is not an end in itself. He has come to lead to Christ, and all who wish to respond to God must now turn to Christ.

Apparently, even John the Baptist's own disciples were having trouble accepting this; only two of his disciples left the ranks to follow Jesus (Jn 1:35–39). Andrew was one; the other remains anonymous. Many scholars believe that this unnamed disciple is the Beloved Disciple himself, which would explain the concern about the relationship between the disciples of John the Baptist and Jesus in the Fourth

Gospel. The narrative goes on to report the calling of Simon, Philip, and Nathanael. The renaming of Simon to Peter (meaning "rock") is interpreted variously, but it at least points to the life-changing character of Jesus.

Given the expectations surrounding John the Baptist (Jn 1:19–28), his affirmation that Jesus is "the one who is coming after" him is tantamount to a declaration that Jesus is the Messiah. This is the main conclusion arising from the comparison of the two. Additionally, though, statements that Jesus surpasses the Baptist because Jesus "was before" John (Jn 1:15, 30) imply Christ's pre-existence. The picture of Jesus as the Messiah, according to John's testimony, involves claims of transcendence not normally associated with other views of the Messiah.

The Messianic Titles of Chapter 1

All of the titles assigned to Jesus in verses 29–51—"Lamb of God," "Messiah," "Anointed," "King of Israel," "Son of God," "Son of Man"—say the same thing: "Messiah." Examined separately, they say even more about the character and function of this Messiah.

The Lamb of God

Twice John the Baptist heralds Jesus as "the Lamb of God" (Jn 1:29, 35). The exact phrase, "Lamb of God," is not found anywhere else in Scripture, but the figure of the lamb is rich in symbolism in Judeo-Christian thought. In the formal institution of the Levitical system, the sacrifice of a lamb provided atonement for sin. Further, the Passover lamb, though not a sacrifice for sin, symbolized deliverance from evil. Still yet another relevant image is the lamb to which the Suffering Servant of the Lord is likened (Isa 53:7). Finally, in certain Jewish apocalyptic circles, the Messiah was described as a powerful horned lamb, or ram, who would bring about the judgment of the wicked and the salvation of the righteous in a decisive way to end the present age and begin the new age.

This eschatological, messianic interpretation is the dominant one in the context of John 1, although it contains elements of the other imageries. Likely several concepts of the lamb are combined into one picture of a Messiah who brings eschatological judgment and deliverance by offering himself to remove our sin.

Messiah, The Anointed, The King of Israel

Other designations in chapter 1 of John—"Messiah" (Jn 1:41), "Anointed" (Jn 1:41), "him about whom Moses in the law and also the Prophets wrote" (Jn 1:45), and "King of Israel" (Jn 1:49)—should all be regarded as simple messianic claims. They each refer to the same figure, but in varied ways, according to different Jewish messianic expectations. There are emphases on God's choice of Jesus, the fulfillment of Old Testament promises, and royal rule, but the reader of the Gospel is not allowed to linger with any one of these ideas as applied to Jesus. John has his own concept of the Messiah to relay by means of a more appropriate title.

Son of God

We might assume that when both John the Baptist and Nathanael call Jesus "Son of God," we have the paramount designation for Jesus. After all, are we not to associate a claim to Jesus' divinity with the use of this particular title? Perhaps not in this context. The idea of divinity in an ontological sense was infused into the title "Son of God" in the early church as Greek thought permeated the church. However, in Jewish circles it was used to speak of the nation of Israel as a whole, the progeny of David, the coming Messiah, righteous people, miracle workers, and charismatic figures. Generally "Son of God" signified the divine election for a role in salvation history. The obedience of the son to the father and dedication to the task is a recurring theme. Here in Nathanael's single confession "Son of God" parallels "King of Israel." Because of this, and the general messianic context of John 1:19–51, "Son of God" should probably be understood here as a reference to the anointed King of Israel, the Messiah.

Many statements throughout the New Testament indicate that the sonship of Jesus is unique and so the Fourth Gospel is not innovative in this respect. However, John's claim that Jesus is the "only" (*monogenes*) Son of God is conspicuously explicit. The term is used of Jesus by John alone (Jn 1:14,18; 3:16,18; 1 Jn 4:9) and literally means "of a single kind." No one but Jesus is God's Son in the sense that he is. This may explain why John does not say that we can become "sons of God." Instead, we become "children of God" (Jn 1:12 and 11:52).

Son of Man

In the final scene of John 1 Jesus responds to Nathanael's confession of him as Son of God and King of Israel, " . . . you will see heaven opened and the angels of God ascending and descending upon the Son of Man." This statement serves as a climax and as a conclusion to the list of messianic titles. Significantly, this is the one term Jesus himself uses. John 1:51 demonstrates that of all the messianic titles offered for Jesus, "Son of Man" best suits him.

The claim to be Son of Man is different than that inherent in the title "Son of God." Popular theology tends to see in the two titles respective claims to Jesus' full divinity and full humanity. Based on the use of the phrase in certain parts of the Old Testament, there is an element of truth to this perspective. However, more is being said than this.

The term "Son of Man" is first used messianically in Daniel 7:13 and from that point it was developed in a number of directions, although it did not have great significance outside of sectarian Jewish apocalyptic circles until Jesus adopted it for his own use. In so doing, Jesus accepts the title of Messiah, but his use of "Son of Man" implies something special about how his hearers are to regard his messiahship. Jesus' own preference for the term "Son of Man" may be due to the ambiguity and mystery of the term itself (Jn 12:34). The messianic title "Son of Man" allowed Jesus to reeducate his hearers about the Messiah.

After the introduction of the Son of Man in John 1:51, later chapters expand upon his origin, function, and destination. In addition to isolated references to the Son of Man (Jn 5:27; 6:62; 8:28; 12:23, 34 and 13:31), the Gospel of John presents extended discourses on Jesus as the Son of Man in 3:12–36 and 6:25–59. Jesus makes the explicit claim that he is the Son of Man (Jn 9:35–38) and he is unique (3:13–31).

A clear picture of Jesus as the Son of Man develops: Jesus, the unique Son of Man, is sent down from heaven to save and to judge. Once his earthly work of deliverance is accomplished, God will exalt him by means of the cross. In this act he returns to the Father, leading the way for those who believe.

Conclusion

The Gospel of John has consistently presented Jesus Christ as the unique and necessary mediator between God and humanity. More than that, the prologue to the Gospel makes a clear and unequivocal claim for his eternal deity and his role as creator and sustainer. The mystery of how he can be God remains a mystery, but it is not a mystery that Jesus was God in the flesh, living in our midst. As the Logos, Jesus Christ is God revealing himself to human beings.

John 1:19–51 presents Jesus as the fulfillment of Jewish messianic hopes. Only in John is the term "Messiah" forthrightly used of Jesus, and the announcement is sounded several times in various ways in the opening chapter of the Gospel. Nevertheless, John does have his own version of the "messianic secret," for even in the midst of such open admissions of Jesus' messiahship, only a few are able to discern in what sense he is the Christ, as we will discover in the following chapters of the Gospel.

STUDY QUESTIONS

1. Besides the Gospel of John, where else do we find similar teachings about the "Logos" or "Word" of God? How does John differ from these?

2. How is the Logos related to creation?

3. How is the Logos related to God?

4. How is the Logos related to humanity?

5. According to John, who were the first two disciples to follow Jesus?

6. List the messianic titles found in John 1.

7. What four images could be behind the phrase "Lamb of God"?

8. Is the quality of divinity necessarily implied in the Jewish use of the title "Son of God"? What seems to be the main emphasis when this title is used? How is it used here in John 1?

9. What is Jesus' title of choice for himself? Why do you think he chose it? What picture does he convey in his use of it?

Chapter 3

NEW BEGINNINGS: FOR THE JEWS
(John 2–3)

Introduction

At the outset of his public ministry, Jesus' words and deeds mark a new beginning. He fulfills the old order and initiates a new spiritual life, offered to all who can accept it in faith, regardless of gender, race, or social status. Because of the special relationship the Israelites have had with God in the past, the new order is described first as it applies to Judaism and then as it applies to the rest of the world. This chapter will focus on the inauguration of the new order for Israel, while chapter 4 will apply the new beginning to the rest of the world.

The new beginning is announced through a miracle Jesus performs: he changes some water into wine at a wedding feast. The reader is told "Jesus did this, the first of his signs, in Cana of Galilee, and revealed his glory; and his disciples believed in him" (Jn 2:11). In this way, the author introduces a major vehicle for the revelation of Jesus: the sign.

Seven miraculous works are found in the first half of John which share specific qualities characterizing them as "signs" (see box). Throughout the Bible the number seven symbolizes completion or perfection, so it is noteworthy that seven signs are selected from many miracles which Jesus performed (note Jn 20:31). The reason why these particular incidents were selected is also profound; the signs themselves have specific revelatory significance on a number of levels.

Superficially, the signs of Jesus have an objective marvelous character which can elicit saving faith, revealing the lordship of Christ over space, time, nature, suffering, and death (Jn 2:11,23; 4:53–54; 6:14; 9:38; 11:27 and 45).

THE SEVEN SIGNS OF JESUS

1. Changing water into wine (2:1–11)
2. Healing a royal official's son (4:46–54)
3. Healing a paralytic (5:1–15)
4. Multiplication of loaves (6:1–15)
5. Walking on the sea (6:16–22)
6. Healing a man born blind (9)
7. Raising Lazarus from the dead (11)

On a deeper level, the signs reveal specifics about the person and work of Christ. Jesus himself provided the impetus for interpreting the signs christologically. After he had fed the five thousand in John 6 (the fourth sign), Jesus becomes frustrated with the lack of insight among the crowd, and he says:

> . . . you are looking for me, not because you saw signs, but because you ate your fill of the loaves. Do not work for the food which perishes, but work for the food that endures to eternal life, which the Son of Man will give to you . . . (Jn 6:26–27).

The miraculous multiplication of loaves had some effect on one level: the people believed that Jesus was the prophet (Jn 6:14). However, Jesus wanted to show by his actions the truth that he is the bread of life which has come down from heaven (Jn 6:33). All of the signs, often with accompanying discourses, make specific statements about the nature and work of Christ. Let us now turn to the first sign to see what it proclaims about him.

The Changing of Water into Wine (Jn 2:1–12)

At Jewish weddings, large jars of water were provided for use in Jewish purification rituals. Ceremonial practice dictated that servants would wash the guests' hands and feet upon arrival. Stricter, more religious people would also return to the purification reservoirs between each course of the feast. At the wedding that Jesus and his disciples attended, these waterpots became the focus.

When told by his mother that the wine had run out, Jesus re-

MANIFESTATIONS OF THE "GLORY OF GOD" IN THE OLD TESTAMENT

God manifested his presence through his "glory" at pivotal moments in the life of Israel, particularly during the Exodus. For example, the glory of God was seen in the cloud by day and the pillar of fire by night:

The Lord went in front of them in a pillar of cloud by day, to lead them along the way, and in a pillar of fire by night, to give them light, so that they might travel by day and by night. Neither the pillar of cloud by day nor the pillar of fire by night left its place in front of the people (Ex 13:21–22).

. . . as Aaron spoke to the whole congregation of the Israelites, they looked toward the wilderness, and the glory of the Lord appeared in the cloud. The Lord spoke to Moses and said, . . . (Ex 16:10–11).

Then Moses went up on the mountain, and the cloud covered the mountain. The glory of the Lord settled on Mount Sinai, and the cloud covered it for six days; on the seventh day he called to Moses out of the cloud. Now the appearance of the glory of the Lord was like a devouring fire on the top of the mountain in the sight of the people of Israel (Ex 24:15–17).

sponded, "Woman, what concern is that to you and me? My hour has not yet come" (Jn 2:4). This cryptic reply, which should not be taken as a harsh treatment of Mary, leaves the reader expecting no further action from Jesus yet also wondering about his coming hour. Unexpectedly, however, Jesus responds with the first sign: he changes the water in the jars to wine. The dramatic foreshadowing of the hour has begun. Jesus "revealed his glory; and his disciples believed in him" (Jn 2:11).

The phrase "glory of God" is a specialized technical reference to God's eternal mode of existence which manifests itself visibly at strategic moments in the plan of salvation (see box). The same language that is used to describe the presence of God in the Exodus is used of Christ. The usage is more fully developed in the rest of the Fourth

Gospel, but at least we can understand the reference to glory in John 2:11 as indicating the presence of God in this act of Jesus.

At a deeper symbolic level, this first sign effectively connects the wine of Jesus to the water of the old order of Judaism. In this respect, the description of six stone waterpots is significant. The waterpots of the Jewish laws of purity have been replaced with the wine of Christ. The symbolism of the number seven suggests that the number six may be interpreted symbolically as something incomplete, unfinished, or imperfect. That the waterpots were made of stone may also be important: according to the laws of purity in the Jewish legal collection called the Mishnah, the impermeability of stone was preferable to baked clay. In other words, even the best that the Jewish purification system can offer is superseded by Jesus.

There is more significance here. Jesus filled the waterpots with wine right to the brim, making between 120 and 130 gallons of wine! Besides the sheer quantity, its premium quality drew comment: it is the best, the kind a host would use to begin a celebration, not end it (Jn 2:10). The details teach us that Jesus is beginning a new era, abundantly better than anything that has gone before.

That Jesus brings the new beginning is now clear, but how he accomplishes it is yet to be clarified. The rest of the chapter relates the death and resurrection of Jesus to the process of a new beginning.

The Cleansing of the Temple (Jn 2:13–25)

The revelation of Jesus builds upon the unexpected and the ambiguous, a strategy continued in Jesus' actions and words in the temple. The fulfillment of Jesus' saving ministry is associated with two acts of violence: one, at the actual temple in Jerusalem, happens now; the other, on the "temple" of the body of Jesus, will happen three years in the future.

The outburst in the temple is recorded in all four Gospels, but in the Synoptics it occurs in the last week before the death of Jesus. Although scholars are divided on the historical placement of this event, it seems most likely that it happened near the end of Jesus' career. As in the Synoptics, John links the temple cleansing to the arrest and death of Jesus, but by placing it at the beginning of Jesus' career he shows that Jesus consciously brought on his crucifixion from the outset of his public ministry.

Sacrifices themselves were not the cause of Jesus' anger; he was disturbed by the business enterprises in the temple area. Since Ro-

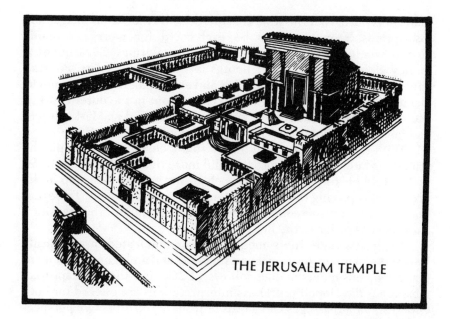

THE JERUSALEM TEMPLE

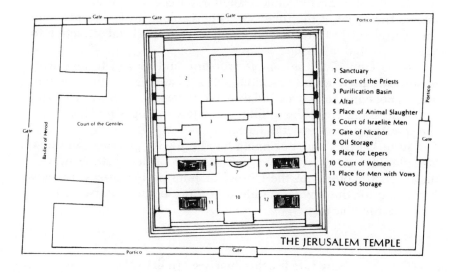

1 Sanctuary
2 Court of the Priests
3 Purification Basin
4 Altar
5 Place of Animal Slaughter
6 Court of Israelite Men
7 Gate of Nicanor
8 Oil Storage
9 Place for Lepers
10 Court of Women
11 Place for Men with Vows
12 Wood Storage

THE JERUSALEM TEMPLE

man coins bore what the Jews considered to be idolatrous images and inscriptions, money had to be exchanged for more acceptable currency before it could be used for temple offerings. Consequently, money changers set up their booths in the temple courts. Pilgrims could also buy their sacrificial birds and animals here. Such commercial activities should not have been carried out in the outer court; it was to be a place of prayer for the Gentiles (Mk 11:17). Market forces had encroached upon worship and provoked Jesus' reaction.

With his actions, Jesus did more than "cleanse" the temple: he sealed his fate. With his words, he did more than explain his actions: he foretold his future. The temple cleansing was the first step in the process of replacing the whole system of temple sacrifices. The eventual death and resurrection of Jesus would complete the transition from the old order to the new.

In this passage, the symbolism is communicated in a typically Johannine manner. Jesus makes a shocking and ambiguous statement (Jn 2:19), misunderstanding follows (2:20), and then the spiritual message is developed (2:21). As interpretations are offered for both Old Testament passages and words of Jesus, a retrospective perspective is betrayed by such statements as " . . . his disciples remembered . . ." (Jn 2:17, 22). These community reminiscences guide the reader into the second level of understanding. Of course, not all who witnessed the event at the time saw its christological significance, and the attitude of Jesus to those with merely a superficial attraction to him is reflected in verses 23–25.

Jesus embodied the temple worship, and he had to be put to death and raised again to facilitate ultimate atonement and worship. He did not come to destroy Judaism, but to make possible its true and full expression. He is the fulfillment of Jewish hopes for those with the sensitivity to accept it in faith.

Jesus Christ's new beginning for the Jewish people, up to now considered at a corporate level, can also be considered at the individual level. Chapter 3 of the Gospel of John particularizes the new beginning for the Jew in the life of a representative person among Judaism: the Pharisee.

New Life for the Pharisee (Jn 3:1–21)

When Nicodemus comes to Jesus, he comes as one who, in spite of all his religious credentials, turns to Jesus for the saving revelation. Even a member of the most devout of the Jewish sects must come to

Jesus for his new beginning. His influential seat on the most powerful religious council, the Sanhedrin, does not preclude his need for a spiritual rebirth.

Thanks to Nicodemus' private encounter with Jesus, we are introduced to John's main metaphor for salvation: eternal life. According to the Gospel of John, eternal life begins in the life of an individual when he or she is "born from above" by the Spirit (Jn 3:3–7). The language of rebirth in the interchange between Nicodemus and Jesus is typically rich in double-meaning and symbolism. The Greek adverb *anothen*, which modifies the verb "be born" in John 3:3 and 7, can actually have two meanings in its context: "from above" and "again."

Consistent with John's dualism, which contrasts what is above with what is below, birth into eternal life comes "from above." One who is born from above is realigned with Jesus. Being born "again" is related; rebirth marks, for the individual, the new beginning Jesus came to bring.

Another dual-meaning analogy in this paragraph elaborates the nature of birth into eternal life. Nicodemus misunderstands Jesus to be speaking about physical birth (Jn 3:4). In correction Jesus states, " . . . no one can enter the kingdom of God without being born of water and Spirit. What is born of the flesh is flesh, and what is born of the Spirit is spirit" (Jn 3:5–6).

"Born of water" is difficult to understand. Water could symbolize procreation, birth, repentance, purification, the word of God, or baptism. Jesus either starts at the point of Nicodemus' misunderstanding, or he makes a new assertion with his use of water imagery. In either case, being born of water is closely tied to being born "of Spirit," the main idea developed by the narrative. The word translated "spirit" (*pneuma*) is also the word for "wind" in Greek. Consequently, in verse 8 we read:

> The wind [*pneuma*] blows where it chooses, and you hear the sound of it, but you do not know where it comes from or where it goes; so it is with every one who is born of the Spirit [*pneuma*].

The intangible nature of spiritual rebirth is likened to the unpredictable influence of the invisible wind. The Spirit of God works mysteriously to begin a life directed and empowered from above.

Nicodemus appears not to understand the spiritual truths being offered him (Jn 3:9) and Jesus' words in John 3:10–12 repeat a pattern of interaction common in the first twelve chapters of the Gospel;

people cannot accept even the most basic claims of Christ when confronted by them. However, the encounter with Christ had some positive impact on Nicodemus, for he later challenged the Jewish religious authorities to give Jesus a fair trial (Jn 7:50–52) and even helped prepare the body of Jesus for burial (Jn 19:38–42). If, as it seems, he became a secret follower of Christ along with others such as Joseph of Arimathea (Jn 19:38), then we must conclude that there was some latitude in the Johannine perspective on belief and discipleship.

The dialogue with Nicodemus evolves into a discourse on the Son of Man, first mentioned in John 1:51. Now we have some further teaching on his origin, function, and destination. John 3:13 states, "No one has ascended into heaven except the one who descended from heaven, the Son of Man." The extended discourse that follows separates Jesus from all other human beings.

The Son of Man is the only one who has first come down from heaven to ascend back again. The most any other person could ever claim was an ascension to heaven from an earthly origin. Inversely, the Son of Man has been sent from his heavenly origin to fulfill an earthly mission. While on earth, he is described as "revealer" (3:13, 32, 34), "Savior" (3:13–16, 12:23), "the bread of life" (6:27, 53), and "judge" (3:18–21, 36; 5:27), the different aspects of his earthly work. The cross has revelatory significance and salvific meaning because it exalts and glorifies the Son of Man in his return to the Father.

The Best Man and the Bridegroom (Jn 3:22–36)

This final section of the third chapter of John recapitulates some of the main themes related to John the Baptist and the beginning of Jesus' ministry. Based on its geography and timing, we can conclude that the Fourth Gospel narrates an earlier period in Jesus' ministry than reported in the Synoptics. At this early stage, the continued allegiance of disciples to John the Baptist needed to be addressed, especially as it related to baptism.

Both John the Baptist and Jesus baptized at the same time, although John 4:2 implies that Jesus delegated the actual act of baptizing to his disciples. John the Baptist's baptism was to be seen as a preparation, and not substitution, for that of Christ. The emphasis on baptism may lead us to conclude that the words "born of water" (Jn 3:5) are indeed a reference for the need to be baptized in the name of *Jesus*.

The wedding imagery, used to full effect to transfer allegiance to Christ, can be compared to similar pictures of Christ and his bride, the church, in other parts of the New Testament. Further, the language would have invoked associations with the Old Testament picture of Israel as the bride of God. God has a new bride—those who commit themselves to the true bridegroom, Jesus Christ. The best man, John the Baptist, can only be happy that the bridegroom now has come to take his bride. His attitude is an example to all who might otherwise feel a sense of loss over the union between Christ and his church.

Again, the dualism of "above and below" is highlighted. Only Jesus Christ can bear witness to heavenly things, for only he has come from heaven and only he has been given the Spirit without measure to speak the word of God (Jn 3:31–34). Unfortunately, not all accept his testimony. A grim warning is sounded for those who cannot receive Christ (Jn 3:36).

At this point, we should note the "realized" eschatological perspective of the Gospel of John. John 3:36 speaks about having eternal life *in the present* and having the wrath of God *remain* on those who do not accept Jesus now. Previously John 3:18 asserted: "Those who believe in him are not condemned; but those who do not believe are condemned already . . ." More so than any other New Testament writer, the fourth evangelist sees our eternal destinies as beginning to be realized when we make our decision for or against Christ.

Conclusion

In sign and discourse, John 2–3 relates the new beginning Jesus brings for the people of Israel. In four highly symbolic episodes, the inauguration of the new order of salvation is described. The best that Judaism can offer does not even approximate, in quality or extent, what Jesus now brings. The sacrificial system of Judaism must realign itself under the ultimate sacrifice in Jesus. Even the Jewish religious leaders stand in need of his gift of life. God has chosen a new bride whose vows are made to her Lord Jesus Christ.

We need to bear in mind the historical context of the fourth evangelist when he speaks of Judaism. Comments throughout the Gospel reveal an early conflict with Jewish religious leaders (e.g. Jn 3:11) and most scholars now believe that Johannine Christians were among the first to be expelled from the synagogue (cf. Jn 9:22; 16:1–4). We will note that throughout the Gospel statements about "the

Jews" are directed specifically against the religious authorities who rejected Jesus' teachings and sought to kill him. However, Johannine Christianity remains indebted to Judaism, in general, for much of its theological reflection on Christ. Jesus is seen to be the fulfillment of Jewish hopes.

From John's perspective, because Jesus came to fulfill the Jewish system, opposition from some was inevitable. In fact, this very opposition is used by God to complete the work of Christ. Those who cannot accept the claims of Christ are not outside of the realm of God; they are held accountable for their response to his revelation.

STUDY QUESTIONS

1. Illustrate from an event in Jesus' career how his actions can be interpreted on more than one level.

2. What does the water in the jars symbolize in John's first sign? What does the wine symbolize?

3. To what does the "glory of God" refer in the Old Testament? How is this motif developed in the Gospel of John?

4. Summarize in your own words the main teaching of the changing of the water into wine.

5. What effect did the cleansing of the temple have upon the ministry of Jesus?

6. What relationship did Jesus' mission have to the Jewish sacrificial system?

7. What two words with double meanings are used in the dialogue with Nicodemus? How are the double meanings related?

8. Compare and contrast baptism by John the Baptist to baptism by Christ.

9. When, according to John, do we enter into eternal life?

Chapter 4

NEW BEGINNINGS: FOR THE WORLD
(John 4)

Introduction

In the fourth chapter of John we see how the offer of a new beginning moves beyond the religious borders of Judaism, through the "intermediate" position of Samaritanism, to the Gentile world.

While Jesus and his disciples ministered to those in Judea, and as his disciples continued to baptize in Christ's name, the news of his success spread. Not all accepted it as good news, but again Jesus uses opposition to accomplish his work. The threat posed by Pharisaic concern prompts Jesus to advance, and not retreat (Jn 4:1–3).

At the Well in Samaria (Jn 4:4–42)

As we proceed through it, John's Gospel takes on a more dramatic structural flair (see box). Commentators have long recognized the way in which the story of Jesus at the well in John 4:4–42 is much like a two-act play. Besides the main story on the front stage, a subplot is developed on a back stage in both acts. A grand finale, with its final chorus, brings closure to all the stories. Some have suggested that the drama develops the standard features of betrothal scenes common to the Hebrew narrative: a future bridegroom travels to a foreign land, he encounters a woman at a well, water is offered, the woman hurries home to report the stranger's arrival, and the bridegroom is then invited to the future father-in-law's home, sealing the betrothal. Jacob's own betrothal follows the same general lines (Gen 29) as this scene in John 4, now at *Jacob's* own well.

Whether or not the fourth evangelist intended to structure his narrative as a "betrothal" play in a figurative sense, it is a useful

29

JESUS AND THE SAMARITANS

Traveling on their way from Judea to Galilee, Jesus and his disciples stop to rest at noon at Jacob's well outside of Sychar, in Samaria (Jn 4:1–6).

<table>
<tr><td>Front Stage</td><td>Back Stage</td></tr>
</table>

Act One
(Jn 4:7–26)

Jesus and the Samaritan woman talk at Jacob's well outside of Sychar. She discovers the source of "living water," the nature of true worship, and, finally, the Messiah.	(In Sychar, the disciples are purchasing food from the townspeople.)

Act Two
(Jn 4:27–38)

The disciples join Jesus and the woman at the well. He teaches them about their expanding mission in God's "harvest."	(The woman returns to town and tells her neighbors about Jesus. They go out to invite Jesus to stay with them in town.)

Grand Finale
(Jn 4:39–42)

After two days with Jesus, many Samaritans believe in him. They proclaim him "Savior of the world."

---

perspective. Act One dramatizes some aspects of the character of Christ, his gift of the water of eternal life, and the nature of true worship, especially as they relate to the Samaritan people. Act Two continues to develop the character of Christ, also commenting on the nature of the Christian mission to the world. The finale represents the union of Christ with his new Samaritan family.

Before the story can start, the stage must be set. Verses 3–6 tell

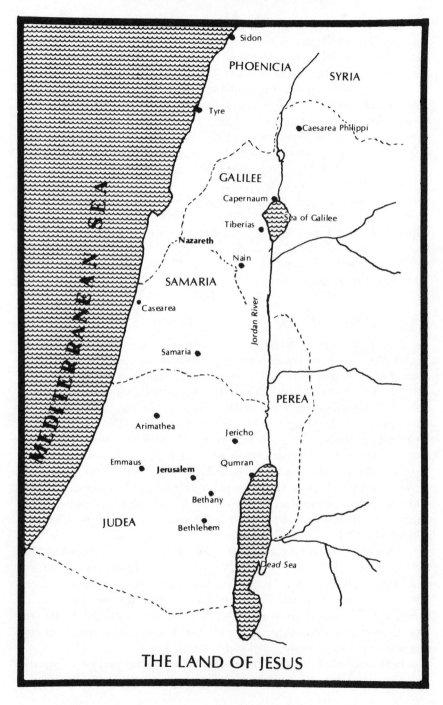

THE LAND OF JESUS

the reader how Jesus arrived at a renowned well in the district of Samaria. The well, previously owned by the patriarch Jacob, still exists today. It is located at the foot of Mount Gerizim just outside of Shechem, about thirty miles north of Jerusalem.

Samaritan descendants from the tribe of Joseph belonged to a strict religious sect. These Samaritans differed sharply from their Jewish cousins on two main points: their choice of the holy mountain of God for worship and their view of the Torah. Basically, the Samaritans believed that the Jews had revised the Torah to diminish the status of Mount Gerizim, in favor of Jerusalem. Consequently, the Samaritans adopted their own version of the Pentateuch. The rivalry between Samaritan and Jew was so strong that they avoided contact with one another, even to the point that Jews would detour around Samaria when traveling between Galilee and Judea (Jn 4:3,4,7; Mt 10:5; Lk 10:52).

This is the backdrop for the introduction of Johannine Christianity to the Samaritan world.

Act One: Jesus and the Woman (vv. 7–26)

The curtain rises at noon. A weary Jesus is sitting alone in the heat of the day. Along comes a woman to draw some water. Jesus asks her for a drink and the truth unfolds in the ensuing dialogue.

The humanity of Jesus shows in a few of the otherwise incidental details of the narrative. He was "tired out by the journey" and had to sit and rest (Jn 4:6). In spite of whatever other agenda he had, when he asked the woman for a drink he was really thirsty. There is no room in this passage for a Gnostic view of Christ which protects him from human suffering. On the other hand, his unity with God is also displayed: Jesus had special knowledge of the woman's domestic history and present relationship (Jn 4:17–19). Such insight, reminiscent of earlier manifestations (Jn 1:42,47; 2:24–25), tells the woman that Jesus is more than he at first seems.

That Jesus even spoke to the Samaritan woman is significant, as the Gospel itself stresses (Jn 4:9,27). Not only did Jews go out of their way to avoid Samaritans, but the rabbis taught that Jewish men were not to greet women in public. Jesus did not share this perspective. To the chagrin of his disciples (Jn 4:22) Jesus transcended social, religious, racial, and sexual barriers all in this one interchange. Everyone stood with the same need in his sight.

In order to minister to the woman, the Johannine Jesus employs the method he used with Nicodemus: he makes an ambiguous statement and capitalizes on the consequent misunderstanding to present a discourse on the nature of eternal life. After their initial words to each other, Jesus says: "If you knew the gift of God, and who it is that is saying to you 'give me a drink,' you would have asked him and he would have given you living water" (Jn 4:10). The phrase "living water" commonly denoted "fresh" or "running" water and so, with only a deep well of still water nearby, the woman's concern about where Jesus will get the "living" water is appropriate. However, Jesus is not speaking merely of running water. Again we need to look below the surface to see where Jesus is going.

Two phrases in John 4:10 give a clue for interpretation. The first, "the gift of God," was used in rabbinic writings to describe the supreme gift: the Torah. Certainly this was a sentiment the Samaritans shared with the Jews. Likewise, "living water" was also used of the Torah; moreover, the simple term "water" frequently represented the Torah in midrashic allegories. Since the Torah was *the* important revelation of God for the Samaritans, Jesus, in effect, presented himself as the new source of God's saving revelation for both the Jews and Samaritans.

Jesus' word -- his saving revelation -- is the living water. Such a claim takes on more import in light of Jeremiah 2:13 and 17:13, which state that God is the fountain of living water (see box). Inasmuch as Jesus is consistently presented by John as the very embodiment of the saving revelation, he is both the fountain of living water and the living water itself.

More than that, the mention of "living water" brings the Holy Spirit into the picture. We've already read in John 1:33 how Jesus has come to baptize in the Holy Spirit. In John 3:5, the close connection between water and Spirit is again made. However, the most direct statement linking this water with the Spirit is found in John 7:37–39:

> . . . Jesus . . . cried out, "Let any who is thirsty come to me, and let the one who believes in me drink. As the Scripture has said, 'Out of the believer's heart shall flow rivers of living water.' " Now he said this about the Spirit, which believers in him were about to receive . . .

Further, in John 14–16 we will see that the Holy Spirit is to function as the presence of the ascended Jesus in the life of the believer. Saving revelation, Holy Spirit, Jesus Christ: all of these are

"LIVING WATER" IN JEWISH THOUGHT

The prophet Jeremiah provides the most direct parallel to the references to living water found in John 4:

> [Thus says the Lord] . . . my people have committed two evils:
>> they have forsaken me,
> the fountain of living water,
>> and dug out cisterns for themselves,
> cracked cisterns
>> that can hold no water (Jer 2:13).

> O hope of Israel! O LORD!
>> All who forsake you shall be put to shame;
> those who turn away from you
>> shall be recorded in the underworld,
> for they have forsaken
>> the fountain of living water, the LORD (Jer 17:13).

In the book of Sirach, Wisdom is personified and identified with the Torah. It is compared to water from various rivers which quench thirst and bring water:

> Those who eat me will hunger for more,
>> and those who drink me will thirst for more.
> Whoever obeys me will not be put to shame,
>> and those who work with my help will not sin.
> All this is the book of the covenant of the Most High God,
>> the law which Moses commanded us
>> as an inheritance for the congregations of Jacob.
> It fills men with wisdom, like the Pishon
>> and like the Tigris at the time of the first fruits.
> It makes them full of understanding, like the Euphrates.
>> and like the Jordan at harvest time.
> It makes instruction shine forth like light
>> like the Gihon at the time of vintage (Sir 24:21–27).

intertwined in the imagery of living water in John, blurring distinctions between them.

Accepting the living water of Jesus results in eternal life. Jesus describes this process in a vivid way: " . . . those who drink of the water that I will give them will never be thirsty. The water that I will give will become in them a spring of water gushing up to eternal life"

(Jn 4:14). With vibrant, natural imagery, Jesus shows how living water, gushing up from the fountain of life himself, is necessary for abundant, eternal life. Jacob's water, and all that it stands for, cannot compare to the living water Jesus offers.

Jacob's well was a symbolic stage setting for talk of more than living water. Being at the foot of Mount Gerizim, it also invited dialogue about true worship. In an attempt to bring the conversation back to a more familiar topic, the woman poses the question about the proper place of worship. Interestingly, in his response, Jesus offers a mild correction in support of the Jewish side of the debate (Jn 4:22). However, Jesus does not leave it at that. In line with what has already been taught in John 2, he goes on to proclaim that both traditions of worship will be superseded in the "hour" (Jn 4:21–23). Foreshadowing what he himself is inaugurating, Jesus says that genuine worshipers will worship God "in spirit and truth."

To worship in spirit is to worship God, for "God is Spirit" (Jn 4:24). This characterization is not to be understood as a metaphysical or ontological claim any more than the phrases "God is love" (1 Jn 4:8) and "God is light" (1 Jn 1:5). Even as we experience God as light and love, we experience God as Spirit. The Spirit of God is not confined to any particular locale. Rather, he infuses all of life and enables worship that transcends traditional limitations. External worship forms, then, are not being ruled out as much as realigned under the Spirit that Jesus introduces.

To worship in truth is to experience God in a real way. "Truth" language in John fundamentally affirms ultimate reality, so worship in truth is genuine worship in the context of genuine life in the Spirit. True worship is not an unreal mystical interlude in an otherwise mundane life of hard reality. True worship completes our experience of reality; in fact, a life with true worship is more real than life without it.

Worship in Spirit and truth must be related to the person of Jesus Christ. While the Holy Spirit is the Spirit of truth (14:16, 15:26, 16:12), Jesus *is* the truth (Jn 14:6). Not only does Jesus offer eternal life through the living water of the Spirit, but through the same Spirit he also makes possible a true encounter with God in worship.

The final words of the woman to Jesus broach the topic of the coming Messiah, and now he openly declares himself to be that Messiah. Jesus uses words loaded with theological significance, at least for the Johannine reader. In the simple admission "I am" (Jn 4:26) Jesus speaks as God speaks, taking upon himself God's name "Yahweh" ("I Am"; see also Jn 8:58; 6:20; and 18:5).

In the dialogue of Act One, the light slowly dawns on the woman, beginning when she developed a thirst for Jesus' living water (Jn 4:15). After he exposes sin and deep need in her life, she declares that he is a prophet (Jn 4:16–19). Finally, our Samaritan woman is ready to leave for the back stage with a tentative faith in Jesus as the Messiah (Jn 4:27–30).

Act Two: Jesus and the Disciples (vv. 27–38)

The disciples enter from the back stage, where they were buying food. They make the surprising discovery that Jesus had been conversing with a woman but the focus quickly shifts from the woman as she exits without her water jar.

Deciding not to voice their astonishment, the disciples instead offer him some of the food they had brought from town. Jesus replies: "I have food to eat that you do not know about" (Jn 4:32). The misunderstanding motif surfaces again. The disciples wonder if someone has brought him food while they were absent, missing completely that Jesus is speaking figuratively.

The food of Jesus has its source in his relationship with God in heaven. Jesus finds his sustenance in doing the will of his Father and completing the Father's work (Jn 4:34). God the Father has given Jesus the Son a particular work to complete (see also Jn 17:4). This "life-work" is not his own, but is a culmination of God's work of creation, revelation, and deliverance. John 5 will expand on this theme of doing God's work as it highlights the unity between the Son and the Father.

Two agricultural proverbs were used by Jesus to elaborate his work. The first one, "Four months more, then comes the harvest" (Jn 4:35), reflects the approximate interval between sowing and harvesting. After sowing, the farmer must wait patiently for the harvest. However, Jesus contrasts the spiritual calendar with the agricultural for there is no more waiting. The fruit for eternal life will not be gathered just among the Jews; the harvest has already started in Samaria.

"One sows, another reaps" (Jn 4:37). This proverb was normally cited cynically to describe life's injustices, but Jesus uses it here to make the encouraging point that the disciples are part of an endeavor that others began. There is no rivalry, only partnership, in the process of sharing the gift of eternal life. In the context of the Gospel timeline, those who ministered to the Samaritans before the disciples include Jesus, John the Baptist (see Jn 3:23; Aenon near Salim is in

Samaria), and even the woman, who is on the other stage sowing a harvest Jesus and his disciples are about to reap.

A problem of interpretation arises in John 4:38 where Jesus says to his disciples "I sent you to reap . . . " Drawing only from John to this point, it cannot be said that the disciples have been sent to reap anything anywhere. Perhaps Jesus, or the evangelist, is speaking retrospectively. A more venturesome suggestion is that we have an allusion to the evangelization of Samaria as recorded in Acts 8:4–24. Note the parallels: Philip sows, Peter and John reap; the living water of the Spirit is received; and worship expands beyond Jerusalem. If this comparison is intentional, then it is an example of the dramatic retelling of an event in the ministry of Jesus as both a precursor and interpretation of later developments in the Christian church.

The story hasn't ended yet. The company on the back stage is being led by the woman to the well.

Grand Finale: The Entire Cast (vv. 39–42)

Clearly the woman was impressed by the insight Jesus had into her life, such that she not only accepted his claim to be the Messiah, but she also persuaded many other townspeople. By doing so she was carrying out the mission Jesus was describing to his disciples; now they were to enter into her labors.

An important observation about belief in Christ can be made here. Some accepted the woman's testimony, but it was only an invitation to a saving relationship with Christ. Verses 41 and 42 tell us:

> . . . many more believed because of his word. They said to the woman, "It is no longer because of what you have said that we believe, for we have heard for ourselves, and we know that this is truly the Savior of the world."

Entrance into eternal life ultimately depends upon belief in the word of Jesus. What is more, such trust cannot exist apart from a personal relationship with Jesus Christ. The mission of disciples of Christ is to bring others to the point that they can meet him for themselves.

The Samaritans declare Jesus the Savior of the world. This is the only time in any of the four Gospels where Jesus is called "Savior," although we do find the term applied to Jesus in the book of Acts and in Paul's letters. Jews never called the Messiah "Savior," but in the

Greek world gods or heroes were given the title. In particular, the Emperor of Rome claimed to be Savior of the world. The Samaritans asserted that Jesus alone was the Savior not just of the Jew or the Samaritan, but of the whole world.

The offer of a new beginning now moves from Samaria to Galilee, where Jesus performs his second sign and gives life to a Roman official's son.

The Royal Official's Son (Jn 4:43–54)

The report of Jesus' entrance into Galilee here is puzzling. We are told "a prophet has no honor in his own country," yet the welcome Jesus received from his own countrymen, the Galileans, is also immediately noted. To solve the difficulty, some have understood Jerusalem to be the religious homeland of Jesus. In this view, disrespect in Judea causes Jesus to move to Galilee. However, such an interpretation neither does justice to the plain meaning of the phrase "in his own country" nor does it take into account his criticism of the Galileans in verse 48: "unless you see signs and wonders, you will not believe." From the Johannine perspective, a reception motivated by a shallow thirst for spectacular "wonders" does not honor Jesus for who he truly is. A deeper faith will have to develop from this superficiality.

As with the first, this sign occurs in Cana of Galilee. A royal official from nearby Capernaum has come to ask Jesus to heal his son. The narrative in John bears striking similarities to the account of the healing of the centurion's son in Matthew 8:5–13 and Luke 7:1–10 and a source-critical analysis suggests that the same event lies behind the different accounts. We may conclude, then, that the royal official was a Gentile, although the Johannine version is not clear in this regard.

What is clear is that Jesus spoke and a dying boy lived. The narrative moves from "death" (vv. 46–49) to "life" (vv. 50–53), with verse 50 as the fulcrum upon which the transition turns: "Jesus said to him 'Go; your son will live.' The man believed the word . . . " The key element in the transition is faith in the word of Jesus. The father starts with a faith based on the wondrous character of miracles (Jn 4:48), moves to a hope for his son based on the word of Jesus (Jn 4:50), and finally arrives at the fuller understanding that Jesus offers life to all people (Jn 4:53).

The word of Jesus is unfettered by spatial, temporal, or racial constraints. Jesus has the power to give a new beginning, both physically and spiritually, to all who can accept his word in faith.

Conclusion

As when a stone is dropped into a still pond, the offer of a new beginning has expanded into ever-widening circles to include the Jews, Samaritans, and Gentiles. Jesus offers a new beginning for the nation and the individual; for the man and the woman; for the body and the spirit.

The new beginning of eternal life is empowered by the Spirit and based upon the truth of Jesus' revelation. Those who can discern Jesus' unity with God the Father in his words and actions must entrust their lives to him. By this, they are born into abundant, overflowing eternal life. From that point on their relationship with Jesus will strengthen, their understanding of his revelation will deepen, their worship of God will widen, and their participation in his mission will heighten.

There will be many others who will see in Jesus bold claims for divinity but this will only be an occasion for their rejection of him. In the next chapter of the Gospel, Jesus clearly exercises divine prerogatives as the Son of God. Those who respond to this in judgment are themselves being set up to be judged.

STUDY QUESTIONS

1. How did the Samaritan view of the Old Testament differ from the Jewish view?

2. What two factors militated against Jesus' initiation of the conversation at the well?

3. How did the woman understand the phrase "living water"? What did "living water" symbolize for the rabbis? What do you think is meant by "living water" here in John 4?

4. What does it mean to "worship in spirit and truth"?

5. Why is the phrase "I am" significant in the Gospel of John?

6. What two proverbs does Jesus use to speak of his ministry here in

John 4? What did they mean in an agricultural setting? How does Jesus change their thrust?

7. What evidence is there that the royal official whose son was healed was a Gentile?

8. Trace three stages in the development of faith in the life of the royal official. What is the turning point of the narrative?

Chapter 5

DOING THE WORK OF GOD:
THE LORD OF THE SABBATH
(John 5)

Introduction

Jesus was on a collision course with the religious authorities in Jerusalem because those Jews saw, in part, the real significance of Jesus' actions. They were not far off the mark when they began to realize that Jesus was doing things that only God should do. Their mistake was to conclude further that Jesus was thereby setting himself up as an autonomous challenger to God.

In John 5, Jesus presents himself as the Son of God who has the authority to work on the Sabbath. The theme of the Son doing the work of his Father is carried on into John 6. Just as the Father led the children in the Exodus and fed them with bread from heaven, Jesus leads a new Exodus and feeds those who are physically and spiritually hungry.

Jesus' claim to be Lord of the Sabbath will be the focus of this present chapter. The issue surfaces at the performance of a healing miracle, the third sign. His action on the Sabbath provokes an exchange between denunciating religious authorities and the self-proclaimed Son of God. In an attempt to interrogate him, the Jewish leaders find out that they themselves are on trial; he will be the judge.

The Healing of the Paralytic (Jn 5:1–18)

Chapter 5 of John records the return of Jesus to Jerusalem. Entering the city from the north through the "Sheep Gate," Jesus encountered a group of infirm people waiting around a pool. The pool, called either *Bethesda* or *Bethzatha* in Aramaic, with its five pillars, is

41

situated near the present day St. Anne's Church. A late addition to the Gospel (Jn 5:4) explains that people believed that the water would be periodically stirred up by an angel and when this happened the first one in the water would be healed.

Unable to walk for 38 years, one paralytic had never been able to make it down to the pool in time to be healed. Nothing suggests that this man was more deserving of mercy than the others at the pool. If anything, there are several hints that he was a dull man of little initiative, faith, insight, moral character, or even gratitude (Jn 5:7,13–15). When Jesus asked him if he wanted to be made well the man did not offer a clear answer; he wasn't expecting to be healed in the water or by Jesus. Even after he was healed, he could not identify his benefactor. Obviously, then, he had no faith in Jesus either before or after the healing. Significantly, John 5:14 links sin and suffering in this man's life, though this is not the case with all who suffer (see Jn 9:3). Later, when the man finally realizes who Jesus is, he promptly reports the "offender" to the authorities.

Jesus, and not the paralytic, is the central figure of the narrative. Again using his characteristic knowledge of people (Jn 5:6,14), Jesus took all the initiative in resurrecting the man to a new quality of life. By the power of Jesus' word alone the man was healed physically. Shortly thereafter, out of a concern for the man's future, Jesus enjoins him to sin no more. While these observations themselves are theologically significant, there is a broader purpose behind the telling of this story.

The broader purpose is found in Jesus' timing. He healed on the *Sabbath* and, what is more, he told a man to carry his mat on the *Sabbath*. In doing so, he contravened Jewish law and brought on the wrath of the religious authorities. Rabbis held that work on the Sabbath was forbidden, and this expressly included such things as the work of healing and carrying your sleeping mat. There was an exception to the rules: God, but only God, continued his sustaining work in the world on the Sabbath. God did not stop giving life and judging those who died on the Sabbath. In light of this background Jesus responds to his accusers with "My Father is still working, and I also am working" (Jn 5:17). To justify his Sabbath activity, Jesus claims to be exercising the authority of God. He does so as God's Son.

The Son and the Father (Jn 5:19–30)

The concept of Jesus as the Son of God is certainly not unique to the Fourth Gospel, but John does refer to Jesus as "the Son" twice as many times as the rest of the New Testament combined! In addition, the Johannine Jesus makes over fifty references to his "Father." The Father-Son imagery in John stresses the intimacy and authority inherent in the relationship between Jesus and the heavenly Father.

The Jews were antagonized by Jesus' shocking statement in John 5:17 "because he was not only breaking the sabbath, but was also calling God his own Father, thereby making himself equal with God" (Jn 5:18). The semitic idiom "making himself equal with God" signified that the Jews thought Jesus was claiming independence from God, which could not be farther from the truth.

In the Johannine style, the misunderstanding introduces a restatement and discourse. Contrary to the conclusion of the Jews, the audience is assured that as the Son of God, Jesus is claiming unity with God rather than independence from him. Jesus explains:

> Very truly, I tell you, the Son can do nothing on his own accord, but only what he sees the Father doing; for whatever the Father does, the Son does likewise. The Father loves the Son, and shows him all that he himself is doing; and he will show him greater works than these so that you will all be astonished (Jn 5:19–20).

In other words, the Son does nothing of his own accord, but works on behalf of the Father. He is not independent; he acts in unity with the heavenly Father. The Son and the Father share the same ultimate will; they want to give life to their people (Jn 5:21).

Resurrecting to new life is the basis for all other descriptions of the common activity of the Father and Son in John 5. The theme of "rising up" at the word of Jesus is developed in both the sign and the discourse. In the sign, Jesus told the paralytic to stand up and take up his mat to walk (Jn 5:8–9,11). The discourse teaches that when all hear the voice of Jesus some will be resurrected to eternal life (Jn 5:21,25–29) and others will be resurrected for judgment (Jn 5:29). The power of Jesus to resurrect to new life is displayed in both the physical and spiritual realm; both now and in the future; and in the lives of both believers and non-believers. It will be manifested even in Jesus' own personal life.

The new life that Jesus brings has its source in God the Father. "For just as the Father has life in himself, so he has granted that Son also to have life in himself . . . " (Jn 5:26). This statement does not mean that Jesus has life, in himself, independent of God; to so conclude would be to make the same mistake as Jesus' accusers. Rather, the Father has given the Son life in himself so that Jesus can directly communicate it to others, even on the Sabbath.

The new life that Jesus offers comes to those who hear and accept his word: we must believe his testimony (Jn 5:24). Due to the context provided by the legal dispute, the case for accepting the life-giving word of Jesus is cast in language of the courtroom. Witnesses come forward, testimonies are heard, and judgment is passed, albeit with a surprising twist in the proceedings.

Testimony and Judgment (Jn 5:31–47)

Jesus has broken the Sabbath. The case for the prosecution is strong. The testimony of the paralytic is not disputed. The facts are substantiated by the defendant's own admission. Jesus' actions are specifically prohibited in the Mishnah. Among 39 other Sabbath interdicts, it specifically condemned the carrying of mats, which is precisely what Jesus commanded (Jn 5:10; cf. *Sabbath* 7:2; 10:5). Further, the work of healing on the Sabbath was also considered a transgression of the Sabbath (Jn 5:16; 7:21). All such prohibitions were built on a scriptural foundation: " . . . the seventh day is a sabbath of solemn rest, holy to the Lord; whoever does any work on the sabbath day shall be put to death" (Ex 31:15). Rabbinic tradition, the Scripture, and even God speaking through Moses were unanimous. Jesus was to be killed.

However, before the case can be closed, Jesus has the chance to address the bench. What began as an apparently formidable suit against Jesus now turns into an overwhelming counter-suit. Because the testimony of one man was not enough to condemn or confirm in a Jewish court (Jn 5:31; 8:18; Deut 19:15; 17:6; Num 35:30), Jesus summons a wide range of witnesses. Even the witnesses for the prosecution become witnesses on behalf of Jesus.

Jesus begins by calling forward someone who, for a while, was highly regarded by the Jews: John the Baptist. He reminds his accusers that even their own priests, Levites, and Pharisees looked to him before he pointed to Jesus (Jn 1:19–28). John's testimony for Jesus still stands and is offered not for the sake of Jesus, but for their own sake (Jn 5:33–34).

Next, Jesus calls for a reconsideration of his own works (Jn 5:36). Here Jesus agrees with his accusers that he is doing the works of God. If God were here, this is what he would be doing. Could it be that he was actually sent by God to act on his behalf? This is Jesus' claim, and the works of Jesus testify to his divine commission.

To support this line of argument, Jesus finally calls the "expert" witnesses which are publicly endorsed by the prosecution. Through the same experts it has already been established that only God should do what Jesus did. If Jesus can now show that these same authorities also support his own right to act this way, then the verdict becomes clear: he is the Son of God.

The first expert is God himself. Jesus says: " . . . the Father who has sent me has himself testified on my behalf. You have never heard his voice and seen his form, and you do not have his word abiding in you, because you do not believe him whom he has sent" (Jn 5:37–38). His adversaries possess the word of God and they've heard and seen Jesus. What is missing is the inner testimony of God in their hearts to confirm the truth of the external witnesses. The Gospel of John teaches that the only way people can experience God so directly is to allow Jesus to abide in them.

Although Jesus did not expect his critics to hear the first expert, at least he could hope for more with his next expert: the Scriptures. After all, the rabbis were the guardians and expounders of Scripture. Jesus argues that the written word of God corroborates his claim to be the Son of God (Jn 5:39). According to all four Gospels, Jesus frequently used Scripture in his debates with the Jews (e.g. Jn 10:34–36). The Fourth Gospel itself often relates how Jesus fulfilled Old Testament passages, particularly in his death and resurrection (Jn 2:22; 7:38,42; 13:18; 17:12; 19:24,28,36,37; 20:9).

At this encounter in particular, the Torah becomes the focus. Moses personifies this final expert (Jn 5:45–47) and he testifies on Christ's behalf. The Jews do not accept even his testimony and so their most venerable expert on the law stands against them. Moses is now their accuser.

All the witnesses have been heard. Jesus is justified by John the Baptist, by his own works, by the Scripture, and by Moses. Behind them all is God. Together they not only acquit Jesus, they exalt him as the Son of God. As such, he commands from worshipers the honor that is due the Father: to detract from Jesus is to dishonor God (Jn 5:23). Jesus does not generate the kind of glory that other people might but rather reflects the Father's own glory (Jn 5:41–44).

Jesus no longer needs supporting testimony. Instead, he offers testimony on behalf of his Father to the world. Those who accept the testimony from the Son of God will enter into eternal life. Those who don't believe his word will be judged.

In a surprising twist the truth comes out. The defendant has actually been the presiding judge throughout this case. Judgment will not be issued by the Jewish religious establishment, but from the Son on behalf of the Father (Jn 5:22,27,30). The Jews would never conceive of bringing a case against God to the courtroom, but this is exactly what they did in their accusations against Jesus. Now they are asked to believe that it is they who are being judged. What is more, there will be no recess or adjournment. Sentencing is imminent.

Condemnation and Acquittal Now

The judgment and deliverance by the Son are present realities. Jesus says "anyone who hears my word and believes in him who has sent me has eternal life, and does not come under judgment, but has passed from death to life. The hour is coming, and is now here, when the dead will hear the voice of the Son of God, and those who hear will live" (Jn 5:24–25). The persistent use of the present tense in these sentences is striking. This is not the only time in the Gospel of John that future expectations are brought into the present. We have already read of the believer who "has" eternal life and the unbeliever who has been "condemned already" (Jn 3:18–21,36). John 12:31 tells us: "Now is the judgment of this world; now the ruler of this world will be driven out" (see also Jn 16:8–11).

Theologians speak of "realized eschatology" to describe this perspective. For the Gospel of John, the future is already realized in Jesus. He confronts all people with his claims and calls for a decision. Those who reject him are judged *now*, those who accept him immediately enter into eternal life. He embodied the new age in his earthly ministry.

It is important to note, however, that the new era is not completely realized in this life. Both the believer and unbeliever still await the culmination of their respective destinies. John 5:28–29 speaks of a future resurrection to either life or judgment and the next chapter of the Gospel sets these events on "the last day" (Jn 6:39–40,44,54; see also 12:46–48).

Conclusion

Jesus took it upon himself to change the life of one of society's most hopeless members. The profound and far-reaching implications of his controversial actions could not be ignored. The healing work on the Sabbath was a sign which forced the Jewish religious leaders to compare Jesus and God.

The parallels between Christ's actions and God's prerogatives point not to a rivalry with the Father, as his critics supposed, but to a unity between the two. Jesus announced in deed and word that he was the Son of God.

The presentation of Jesus as the Son of God establishes the basis for Jesus' mission. The Father has sent his only Son on a mission to share what he has been given to believers. In obedience and dependence, Jesus does the work of God here on earth. There is a unity of knowledge, will, and action between Father and Son. The Son carries the authority of his heavenly Father and represents him fully to humanity.

Jesus backs up his testimony of God with other witnesses and our response now to the evidence decides our eternal future. Accepting his revelation of the Father brings life. Rejecting his revelation brings judgment and condemnation.

The next chapter of the Gospel again has Jesus do the work of God. He leads a new Exodus, walking on the water and offering bread from heaven. The reader must decide whether to follow Jesus and eat the bread of life.

STUDY QUESTIONS

1. Aside from the timing, what does the actual healing of the paralytic say about the character of Jesus and his ministry? What does it say about those to whom he chooses to minister?

2. What was the penalty prescribed for working on the Sabbath?

3. Equality with God can be understood in one of two mutually exclusive ways. What are they? What way did the Jewish leaders take it? What way does John present it?

4. What concepts does the Gospel of John communicate in its use of the Father-Son motif?

5. List six verses in John 5 that speak of resurrection in one form or another.

6. List the witnesses Jesus calls upon to support his case. In what ways do you see them substantiating Jesus' claim to have the right to work on the Sabbath?

7. How is our respect for Jesus related to our worship of God?

8. Define "realized eschatology" and illustrate it from passages in John. How does this relate to our future hope?

Chapter 6

DOING THE WORK OF GOD:
THE BREAD OF LIFE
(John 6)

Introduction

The fourth and fifth signs, both found in John 6, point to Jesus as the one who leads the second Exodus. As God fed the people of Israel with manna while they were wandering in the wilderness, Jesus feeds his followers (Jn 6:1–15). The walking on the water (Jn 6:16–22) draws on the imagery of the crossing of the Red Sea. The extended discourse of John 6:25–59 reflects further on the manna motif, focusing upon God's ultimate provision through the Son of Man. Finally, the response of Jesus' hearers in John 6:60–71 challenges the readers of the Gospel.

Although the Exodus allusions are easily discerned, there are several interpretive difficulties in John 6. The final three sections (i.e. vv. 35–50, 51–59, and 60–71) do not stand easily together. Incongruities and inconsistencies, such as the exhortation to eat the flesh and drink the blood of the Son of Man in 6:51–58 and the disparagement of the flesh in 6:63, have prompted some scholars to suggest that either vv. 51–58 or 60–71 are late editorial additions. There is wide disagreement as to which section does not belong, and most of the debate centers around whether sacramental theology is present. Does chapter 6 refer directly to the eucharist or not? A case can be argued either way.

While it is clear that the Gospel did undergo a process of composition, we should not resort to a "cut and paste" method of reconstruction in attempts to arrive at a proper interpretation of the text. Most of the chapter is a homiletical development in the Jewish style of a quote from Scripture: "He gave them bread from heaven to eat" (Jn

6:31; cf. Ex 16:15 and Ps 78:24). Our evaluation of the internal unity of the chapter depends to a considerable extent on our interpretation of its eucharistic overtones. We are probably wrestling with some of the same issues as the first hearers, for they too found Jesus' teaching "difficult" (Jn 6:60).

Into the Wilderness (Jn 6:1–15)

The new Exodus begins as Jesus leads a crowd into the wilderness by the seashore (Jn 1–2). Eventually he arrives at the foot of a mountain and ascends in the manner of Moses (cf. Jn 6:3 and Ex 3–4; 19; 24; 31–34). The mention of the Passover in verse 4 strengthens associations with the Exodus. Looking over the approaching multitude, Jesus prepares to satisfy their physical and spiritual hunger.

All four Gospels contain accounts of miraculous multiplication of loaves (Mt 14:13–21; 15:29–38; Mk 6:31–44; 8:1-19; Lk 9:10–17; Jn 6:1–15). As much as there are strong parallels between the Synoptic accounts and John, the independence of the Johannine account of the feeding of the five thousand is well established. Unique to John are the mention of the Passover, the roles of Philip and Andrew, and the young boy with *barley* loaves and *dried fish*. In addition, compared with the Synoptics, John emphasizes the initiative of Jesus from the beginning to the end of the narrative. While some of these details may have little symbolic significance, several of them combine to give this account its character as a sign (Jn 6:14) relating the manna from heaven (Ex 16) to bread through Jesus.

The comments of verses 5 and 6 are puzzling. John stresses that Jesus already had plans to feed the crowd miraculously, yet he turns to Philip, from nearby Bethsaida (Jn 1:44), and asks him where they might buy enough bread for all. Philip calculates that it would take more than eight months of a laborer's wages to buy enough for everyone. Philip's "test" (Jn 6:6) is actually for the benefit of the readers. We now know the extent of the need and the unlikelihood of meeting it through ordinary means. Andrew's response is similar to Philip's, contrasting the great need and meager resources (Jn 6:9). The words and actions of both disciples present the leader of the new Exodus as the only hope.

Once the context is set, Jesus immediately takes action. He directs the disciples to seat the people. "Then Jesus took the loaves, and when he had given thanks, he distributed them . . . " (Jn 6:11). Because this description is so similar to those used to describe the institution of the eucharist (Mt 26:26; Mk 14:22; Lk 22:19; 1 Cor 11:23–

24), most scholars have assumed a reference to the sacrament. In light of the discourse on the bread of life (Jn 6:25–59), which contains clearer associations with the Lord's supper, a eucharistic interpretation of verse 11 is possible. The case is made even stronger by the observation that John says Jesus "gave thanks" (from *eucharistein* in the Greek) when the Synoptics say "blessed" (*eulogein*).

The main point of this sign is clear: in the face of humanity's greatest need, Jesus alone is an abundant source of life. This teaching is framed in allusions from Exodus 16. Philip is being put to a "test" (Jn 6:6) just as the Israelites were put to a "test" in the giving of the manna (Ex 16:4). As meat followed manna, fish follows bread. The crowd in Galilee ate as much as they wanted (Jn 6:11); the Israelites were allowed to take as much as they needed (Ex 16:8,12,18). Jesus directed the disciples to gather the fragments (Jn 6:12,13) as God directed the Israelites (Ex 16:4,5,16). The reason given for the gathering in John 6:12 is so that none of the fragments will "be lost." The verb is more accurately translated "perish," which correlates with the descriptions of the day's leftover food rotting in Exodus 16:20 (cf. also Ex 16:24). Later, in John 6:27, Jesus contrasts the food that endures to eternal life with that which perishes. The *twelve* baskets, also mentioned in the Synoptics, could connect the church's apostles with the tribes of Israel, although the concept of the twelve apostles as a special group is only a minor theme in the Gospel of John.

The people's response showed they clearly understood the multiplication of bread as a miraculous act of God. They concluded that Jesus was "the prophet who has come into the world" (Jn 16:14). Basing their eschatological hopes on the promise of Deuteronomy 16:15, the Jews awaited a prophet like Moses to usher in the kingdom of God. Some even believed that when this final time came, manna would again be sent.

Excitement mounted. Was the messianic age dawning? Popular Jewish fervor for political liberation quickly centered on Jesus. However, Jesus was more than the prophet like Moses; he was no mere king who would reign in the political realm. He could not allow the crowds to distort his mission, create misunderstanding, and give authorities a legal reason to apprehend him. Consequently, he "withdrew again to the mountain by himself" (Jn 6:15). He would clarify the nature of his mission at another time and place (Jn 6:25–59).

Crossing the Sea (Jn 6:16–24)

John's fifth sign is a fitting complement to the fourth, as it also develops an Exodus motif. By walking on the sea and delivering the

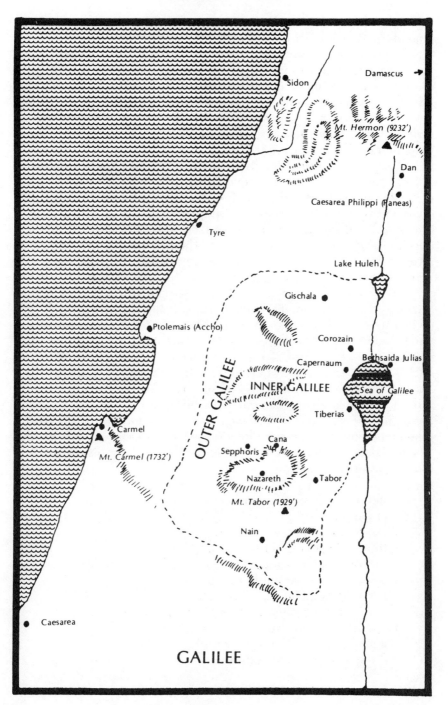

GALILEE

disciples' boat safely to shore (Jn 6:16–21), Jesus reenacts the crossing of the Red Sea (Ex 14:1–15:21). The less detailed description has
less obvious verbal correspondences with the Exodus account, yet a
close examination will yield a profound message.

The setting of the event is carefully and concisely established.
Evening has come and Jesus has not rejoined his disciples; they decide to make a night voyage across the Sea of Galilee to Capernaum
without him. About halfway across the 11 kilometer-wide sea, a storm
hits them.

These descriptive details function much like the testimony of
Philip and Andrew in the previous narrative, presenting the great
need of the disciples and the truly miraculous nature of the sign. John
does not describe the disciples as simply being calmed by the sight of
Jesus walking "along" the sea on the shore; Jesus walked out to them
in the middle of the sea and rescued them. Furthermore, the act of
walking on the water is only part of the miracle; the boat was amaz-
ingly transported to land (Jn 6:21).

Although we can assume that the disciples were afraid while they
struggled in the storm, this narrative only mentions their fear of Jesus;
when they saw Jesus, they were terrified (Jn 6:19). The best way to
understand this fear is to see it in the context of a divine appearance
complete with the use of the divine name "I am" (Jn 6:20, cf. Ex
3:14). When translations here render the statement "I am *he*" they
are supplying a word which is absent in the Greek. The disciples are
struck by the awesome presence of God in Jesus.

The crossing of the Red Sea was also regarded as a powerful
theophany on the water. Psalm 77:16–19, in describing this Exodus
event, speaks of the fear generated by God making his stormy way
through the sea:

> When the waters saw you,
>   O God,
> When the waters saw you,
>   they were afraid;
>   the very deep trembled.
> The clouds poured out like water;
>   the skies thundered;
>   your arrows flashed on every side.
> The crash of your thunder was in the whirlwind
>   your lightnings lit up the world;
>   the earth trembled and shook.

Your way was through the sea,
　　your path, through the mighty waters;
　　yet your footprints were unseen.
You led your people like a flock
　　by the hand of Moses and Aaron.

The sign in John 6:16–24 escalates the presentation of Jesus beyond the previous sign (Jn 6:1–15). Jesus is more than the prophet like Moses, he is exalted as the manifestation of God himself. While the disciples are separated from Jesus, they are in the dark, struggling under their own power against the forces around them. God comes to them through Jesus; when they see and accept him, they are delivered.

After the disciples have landed, the narrative continues with a transition (Jn 6:22–24). This section confirms that the disciples had set sail, without Jesus, in the only boat available. At the same time, it describes the later arrival of more boats which enabled some of the crowd to follow Jesus and his disciples to Capernaum. Embedded in this text is a phrase which, given its context, is striking. The reader is told that boats arrived at the place where the bread was eaten "after the Lord had given thanks" (Jn 6:23).

There are several variant readings of these verses in our most ancient manuscripts, some of which omit the reference to giving thanks (again from *eucharistein*, cf. Jn 6:11). Possibly, scribal copyists found the reference to giving thanks out of context. On the other hand, the jarring effect it has on the reader may have been intended as a bridge from the miraculous feeding to the eucharistic language of the "bread of life" discourse which now follows.

Bread from Heaven (Jn 6:25–59)

The reunion of the crowd and Jesus in Capernaum marks a return to the theme of the first sign. Even though they ate of the bread, the crowd had not perceived the sign, so now it will be explained to them (Jn 6:26–27,36). Still, their experience on the other side of the sea had caused many to wonder if Jesus could be the prophet like Moses. Here, in order to make the comparison between Jesus and Moses, they felt they needed a greater miracle from Jesus. After all, Moses had provided an entire nation with bread from heaven for 40 years! In support of their request for more, the people remind Jesus of Moses'

THE SEVEN "I AM" SAYINGS OF JOHN

1. I am the bread of life (Jn 6:35, 51)
2. I am the light of the world (Jn 8:12, 9:5)
3. I am the gate (Jn 10:7, 9)
4. I am the good shepherd (Jn 10:11, 14)
5. I am the resurrection and the life (Jn 11:25)
6. I am the way, the truth and the life (Jn 14:6)
7. I am the true vine (Jn 15:1, 5)

feat by citing a variation of Psalm 78:24: "He gave them bread from heaven to eat" (Jn 6:31; cf. also Ex 16:15).

Contrary to what the people intended, this quotation is used to correct them. Actually, says Jesus, *God* is the subject of the quotation; God, not Moses, is the one who provided the manna. Now, by offering bread from heaven, Jesus is comparing himself with God and transcending the role of Moses. The audience is challenged to rise above their focus on Moses and transfer their allegiance to Jesus.

Those who wish to eat the bread that gives eternal life must believe in Jesus. Integral to this belief is a recognition of the heavenly origin of Jesus, as indicated by the many references to Jesus having "come down from heaven" (Jn 6:33,38,41–42,48,50–51,58). Further, as one more strong tie to his heavenly Father, Jesus declares "I am the bread of life" (Jn 6:35,51). This is the first of Jesus' seven "I am" sayings in John that have complements for the verb "to be" (see box).

As we've noticed before, the number seven is significant, denoting completion or perfection. In connection with John 4:26 and 6:20, we've already established that the simple phrase "I am" alludes to the one God, Yahweh. Elaborating upon an affirmation of divinity, the "I am" sayings describe his divinity in relation to people.

In declaring "I am the bread of life" Jesus claims to offer the only satisfaction for the spiritually hungry. Just as bread was the staple of life, Jesus is the necessity for spiritual sustenance. The saying and its accompanying discourse teach that Jesus is *himself* the life-giving food, that he is not just its "dispenser," and that the "life" he offers is spiritual and eternal, not just physical and temporal.

The audience in chapter 6 of John is told to "eat this bread." The concept is further developed with the words " . . . the bread which I shall give for the life of the world is my flesh" (Jn 6:51). Further, Jesus enjoins all to "eat the flesh and drink the blood of the Son of Man" (Jn 6:53). Immediately the Christian reader associates these words with the eucharist. Indeed, the first readers of the Gospel of John would surely have made this connection as well since, by that time, they were regularly celebrating the Lord's supper. However, the eucharist would have been unknown by those who heard the words when they were first spoken and so we must look elsewhere for the primary theme. The sacramental allusions are used in the sign and the discourse to make the eucharist itself point to truths concerning Christ and faith in him.

The Israelite Wisdom tradition and Isaiah both provide some explanatory background. Compare the words of Jesus in John 6:35 with the invitation of Wisdom in Proverbs 9:5: "Come, eat of my bread; drink of the wine I have mixed" (cf. also Sir 15:3 and 24:21). In Isaiah also the Lord invites hearers to eat the bread that satisfies (Isa 55:1–2). God's word is described as coming down from heaven, bringing bread to the eater (Isa 55:10–11).

In light of these biblical themes, Jesus, as the bread of life, is primarily to be understood as God's life-giving word. An interesting term is used to describe how we are to "eat" this bread of life. Instead of the usual verb for eating (*phagein*) used throughout this chapter, in John 6:56 we find a word originally used of animals "munching" or "chewing" (*trogein*): "Those who '*chew*' my flesh and drink my blood abide in me and I in them." In a graphic way, we are being called to a total, intimate, involved, and ongoing relationship with Jesus. He has come down from heaven to invite all to partake fully of his incarnation and thus find eternal life that will transcend even physical death. Given John's realized eschatology elsewhere, it is notable that in this discourse eternal life is to be culminated in a "last day" resurrection of individual believers (Jn 6:39–40,44,54).

The Choice Before All Followers (Jn 6:60–71)

Jesus has presented his claims, calling for belief. John 6:60–71 goes on to relate the response of those who have followed him to this point. True disciples are sifted from unbelievers. We have already been told that the "work" we must do to have eternal life is "to believe" in him whom God has sent (Jn 6:29). This belief has been likened to "eating" the bread of life Jesus who has come down from heaven. It is not an easy belief and not all can stomach the bread.

The disciples describe Jesus' words as "difficult" (Jn 6:60) to accept or believe. The sense of the words being offensive, intolerable, or incredible is conveyed, as the question of Jesus in the next verse implies: "Does this offend you?"

Jesus clearly knows why some are offended. John 6:61, 64–65 and 70–71 all imply his foreknowledge, a characteristic of the Johannine Christ. John wants to avoid the conclusion that Jesus has made a mistake in choosing some of his disciples. His words also serve to remind all disciples of the divine initiative that underlies faith (cf. also Jn 6:37–39 and 44).

Jesus responds to the hesitancy of the disciples by proposing a further consideration in verse 62: "Then what if you were to see the Son of Man ascending to where he was before?" This conditional sentence lacks a conclusion, creating a purposeful ambivalence. Along with the disciples, the reader is forced into a decision: if Jesus ascended back into heaven, would he be easier, or harder, to accept?

John 6:63 follows with a typical Johannine statement referring to the life-giving Spirit. However, its antithesis—the flesh—causes interpretive problems. How can Jesus say that the flesh is of no profit after having exhorted his disciples to eat his flesh in order to live forever? In the final analysis, it would appear that the evangelist is simply but effectively calling for a full recognition of the spiritual realm as the source of the eternal life Jesus offers. In the context of eucharistic language, we must go beyond the sign of bread to the spiritual reality of Christ.

Finally the disciples make their choices. John 6:66 describes the actual division of the group of disciples which began with the questioning in verse 60 and was made explicit in verse 64. Many disciples could no longer follow him. The twelve won't also leave, will they? Jesus asks them this question in such a way that, according to John's grammar, a negative answer is expected (Jn 6:67). The emphasis may have been intended to confirm their faith as others were falling away.

For the first time in this Gospel, Peter speaks out on behalf of the disciples. Verses 68–69 make up Peter's three-part answer, which begins with another rhetorical question in response to that of Jesus. Peter replies, "Lord, to whom can we go? You have the words of eternal life. We have come to believe and know that you are the Holy One of God." These words echo Jesus' words of verse 63b: "The words that I have spoken to you are spirit and life." The all-embracing life-giving quality of Jesus' words are obvious to the disciples and, in spite of their difficulty, the twelve have decided to accept his words rather than turn away from Jesus.

The evangelist is clearly distinguishing Peter and the twelve from unbelievers. The use of the verbs "believe" and "know" together is characteristic of John and they exist in either order, so it is unlikely that here a definite development is being described. It is much easier to maintain that the two verbs are practically synonymous in John, often used interchangeably in close proximity to one another.

Not all disciples share in the eternal life Jesus gives, because not all disciples remain attached to Jesus in faith. Some disciples can be described as followers yet uncommitted. There are yet others, such as Judas, who will actually turn on Jesus in betrayal (Jn 6:70–71). In all cases, John makes it clear that divine initiative and sovereignty rules over the course of Jesus' life-giving ministry.

Conclusion

In John 5 and 6 we have seen how Jesus does what his audience would recognize to be the work of God. He works on the Sabbath, something the rabbis insisted that only God should do. He leads the new Exodus, not in the role of Moses, but in the role of God. In the wilderness he feeds the people with bread from heaven. He crosses the sea, delivering his disciples from danger.

The words and actions of Jesus indicate the nature of the relationship he has with his heavenly Father. He has been sent from heaven to act with the Father's authority. In no way is he to be considered a rival to God; rather, the Son acts in complete unity with his Father. Jesus is unique in his relationship to the Father; his divinity distinguishes him from all other human agents in the plan of God. He acts in divine initiative and sovereignty to bring eternal life to those who respond to him in faith.

Much is revealed about humanity's relation to Jesus in these two chapters as well. When people are separated from him, they are not able to deliver themselves from their troubles. They are completely dependent upon him and his initiative. Once he enters into their lives and confronts them, then they are asked to make a choice. Either they accept his word and entrust their lives to him, or they decide to stay on their own. Thus, there are only two groups of people: those who believe Jesus and those who don't. As the Gospel narrative progresses, confrontations continue and the division between belief and unbelief deepens.

STUDY QUESTIONS

1. List all the possible allusions to Exodus events you can detect in this chapter.

2. How would you describe the differences between Moses and Jesus as presented in John 6?

3. What do John 6:20 and 35 have in common? What does this common detail suggest about the person of Jesus?

4. List all the possible allusions to the eucharist you can discern in this chapter.

5. Offer at least three possible backgrounds for the imagery of eating bread used here in the Gospel of John.

6. What do you think is the primary meaning of Jesus' words "eat my flesh"? How does this relate to "believing" and "knowing"?

7. How would you fit the sacramental theology into the teachings of this chapter?

8. In John 6:54 Jesus says "those who eat my flesh . . . have eternal life." In John 6:63 he says "It is the spirit that gives life; the flesh is useless." Are these statements contradictory?

9. What does this chapter say about a future hope?

10. Several verses in this chapter comment on the omniscience of Jesus and divine initiative. List and comment on the function of these statements.

Chapter 7

CONFRONTATIONS:
THE PROVOCATIVE TEACHER
(John 7)

Introduction

A marked change in character occurs with chapter 7 of the Gospel. No longer does Jesus stand uninterrupted, developing a lofty theological treatise for an eager, listening crowd. Instead, he throws himself into a fray of discordant voices, hostile opinions from his brothers, festival crowds, temple police, chief priests, and Pharisees.

The teaching of Jesus is often punctuated by questions, objections, and challenges. We even encounter arguments to which Jesus is not party (e.g. Jn 7:40–52). From this conflict emerge several interwoven themes: belief and unbelief, Jesus' "time," authority and judgment, the origin of the Messiah, the glorification of Jesus, and the giving of the Spirit.

In their context, these themes all reinforce what we've seen in John so far: Jesus is the fulfillment of Israel's faith, specifically here as it is expressed in the Feast of Booths (see box). In presenting himself in this way Jesus provokes a crisis for his hearers, calling them to make a decision. The setting and christological thrust carry on into John 8, where Jesus is compared to the lights of the festal ceremonies.

Even before Jesus arrives at the feast in Jerusalem, some of the themes are introduced.

Is It Time for Jerusalem? (Jn 7:1–13)

In chapter 7 of the Gospel, Jesus is with his brothers in Galilee. We are told that he avoided a return to Judea because the religious authorities in Jerusalem were plotting to kill him. However, the most

59

JEWISH FESTIVALS IN JOHN

There were three Jewish festivals marked by pilgrimages to the temple: the Passover (*Pesah*); the Feast of Weeks (Pentecost or *Shavuot*); and the Feast of Booths (*Sukkot*). In addition to their religious meaning, each feast was associated with an agricultural season.

Of these, two are reflected in the Gospel of John:

The Passover

Held in the spring, the Passover festival celebrates the exodus, when the people of Israel were brought out of slavery in Egypt. The day before Passover (the day of Preparation; cf. Jn 19:14, 31), lambs were slaughtered. As well, the entire household would be cleansed of leaven. Then, using the hyssop plant (Jn 19:29), the blood of the Passover lamb was sprinkled on the doorposts (Ex 12:22).

A special meal of the lamb, unleavened bread, bitter herbs, and wine was observed in remembrance of God's deliverance as he "passed over" the Israelites while striking Egyptian households (Ex 12:13).

John records the Passover celebrations over a three year period (Jn 2:23; 6:4; 13:1). Especially during the Passion narrative (Jn 13–19), he presents Jesus as the Passover lamb slain for the deliverance of God's people.

The Feast of Booths

The Feast of Booths (or Tabernacles) originated as a harvest celebration in the fall, although it became a commemoration of God's protection of the Israelites as they camped during the forty years in the wilderness. Celebrants dwelt in tents, or "booths," around the temple for the eight-day period of the feast.

Every day, a procession made its way to the Pool of Siloam where water was drawn. Then the water would be brought to the temple and poured on the altar. As well, the festal evenings ended with an elaborate lamp-lighting ceremony in the court of the women to celebrate the nocturnal pillar of fire during the Exodus pilgrimage.

During this feast, John shows Jesus as the source of living water in comparison to the waters drawn from the pool and poured out on the altar. Jesus is also the "light of the world." More than the great lamps and many torches which light up the Jerusalem night, and more than a pillar of fire for some Hebrew wanderers, Jesus alone illuminates on an eternal, cosmic scale.

✳ ✳ ✳

During Jesus' time, another festival was celebrated in Jerusalem: the Feast of Dedication (*Hanukkah*). It celebrated the purification of the Temple after the Maccabean revolt of 167 B.C. Following the format of the Feast of Booths, on each day of the festival, another of eight candles on the special candelabra, the menorah, was lit. The festival is mentioned in passing in John 10:22.

popular Jewish festival of the year was about to be celebrated at the temple and Jesus' brothers urged him to attend.

The Feast of Booths (or Tabernacles) originated as a harvest celebration, although it became a commemoration of God's protection of the Israelites as they camped during the forty years in the wilderness. Celebrants dwelt in tents, or "booths," around the temple for the eight-day period of the feast. Besides the erection of tents, two other rituals distinguished this feast. Every day a procession made its way to the Pool of Siloam where water was drawn while the choir would repeat Isaiah 12:3: "With joy you will draw water from the wells of salvation." The procession returned to the temple and, after marching around the altar once, the priest poured the water on the altar. As well, every day of the feast ended with an elaborate lamp-lighting ceremony in the court of the women to celebrate the nocturnal pillar of fire during the Exodus pilgrimage.

The brothers of Jesus suggested that it was time that Jesus showed his miraculous works at a great public gathering in Jerusalem so that he would become widely known. They added that his disciples needed the encouragement of a more open display of miracles. However, the evangelist also tells us that Jesus' brothers did not themselves believe in him (Jn 7:5). This may be John's way of reiterating that faith in Jesus means more than accepting his ability to do the spectacular.

Jesus does not share his brothers' perspective on the timing and nature of his career success. He tells them:

> My time has not yet come, but your time is always here. The world cannot hate you but it hates me because I testify against it that its works are evil. Go to the festival yourselves, I am not going to this festival, for my time has not yet fully come (Jn 6:6–8).

One striking feature of Jesus' response is the way in which Jesus emphasizes his "time." This the first of five references in this chapter to the special timing of an event in Jesus' future (cf. vv. 6,8,30,33 and 39). We first encountered this concept in John 2:11, when Jesus tells his mother "My hour has not yet come" (cf. Jn 7:30 and 8:20). Later, as the cross comes nearer, we will find more references to this hour (Jn 12:23,27; 13:1; 17:1). All are references to Jesus' crucifixion. It will be a time when he returns to the Father (Jn 7:33), is glorified, and bestows the Spirit (Jn 7:37–39).

Jesus says to his brothers "I am not going to this festival" (Jn 7:8) yet in verse 10 we read that he does attend. In order to make the two statements agree, well-meaning scribes have changed some ancient manuscripts to read Jesus saying he's "not yet" going. However, the apparent contradiction can better be alleviated by interpreting the paragraph in its greater context. John may have been trying to stress that Jesus' actions were not dictated by others; he followed only the Father's direction. More specifically, Jesus did not go to Jerusalem at the time and in the manner requested by his brothers. Instead, he went after they did, in private without the fanfare of the miraculous.

What is more, the phrase "not going" in verse 8 is more literally translated "not going up." The Greek word used (*anabaino*) is the same word used in John to speak of Jesus' "ascension" from the cross to the Father (cf. Jn 3:13; 6:62; 20:17). Perhaps the reader is being told subtly that Jesus will deliberately go to Jerusalem to be arrested, crucified, and thus ascend to his heavenly Father: but not now. Indeed, the rest of the chapter repeatedly relates how attempts to arrest Jesus are still unsuccessful (Jn 7:1,26,30,32,44–46). It is not time for *the* fateful trip to Jerusalem.

During the first few days in Jerusalem, even while Jesus remained out of sight, divisions arose among the people concerning him (Jn 7:12). Many people, perhaps even other believers, were aware of the danger in store for Jesus and themselves did not speak publicly of him. Since these people were presumably Jewish, "the Jews" mentioned in John 7:11 and 13 must refer only to the religious leaders who sought to arrest and kill Jesus. They obviously wielded considerable authority in the Jewish community, but it was not of the same nature as the authority exercised by Jesus.

True Authority and Judgment (Jn 7:14–24, 45–49)

Midway through the festival, Jesus begins to teach openly in the temple. Immediately the religious leaders converge upon him. Based on the dialogue of John 7:19–24, the charge of healing the paralytic on the Sabbath still stands against Jesus (Jn 5). The forensic language and rabbinic debate found in John 5 resurfaces, but again Jesus turns the tables on those who would stand in judgment over him.

Besides that of breaking the Sabbath law, other criticisms are leveled against Jesus: He is "deceiving the crowd" (Jn 7:12,47); he has "never been taught" (Jn 7:15); he "has a demon" (Jn 7:20); and, finally, he comes from Galilee and so cannot be either a prophet or the Messiah (Jn 7:27,41–42,52).

On the other hand, even his opponents are astonished with Jesus' teaching (Jn 7:15). Though not trained by a rabbi, he employs rabbinic legal interpretation to argue that the rabbis should allow the healing of a person's whole body on the Sabbath since they allow circumcision on the Sabbath (Jn 7:19–24). Even more commanding than his ability to engage the rabbis in debate was the effect he had on common people. His authority was inherent, not derived; his words immobilized critics and compelled many to believe in him. His impact on the temple police is just one example: When the Pharisees asked them why they did not arrest Jesus as directed, they explained "Never has anyone spoken like this!" (Jn 7:46).

The source of Jesus' power is his relationship with his Father. Jesus, and his teaching, have originated from heaven. He has been sent not to speak on his own behalf, but for God. He seeks God's glorification, and not self-glorification (Jn 7:18). Jesus directly counters each criticism made of him: he's not a deceiver; he is "true, there is nothing false in him" (Jn 7:18). He's not uneducated; he's been taught by God (Jn 7:16,17). He does not have a demon; he has the Spirit (Jn 7:37–39). He does not break the law of Moses; he fulfills it more than his accusers (Jn 7:23). He actually does not come from Galilee; he comes from heaven (Jn 7:16,28–29,33–34).

More than once Jesus appeals to his audience to evaluate his claims and decide what is right. He says, "Anyone who resolves to do the will of God will know whether the teaching is from God or whether I am speaking on my own" (Jn 7:17). After setting forth his case for healing on the Sabbath, he issues the challenge: "Do not judge by appearances, but judge with right judgment" (Jn 7:24).

As Jesus is judged, divisions arise between the people and their leaders, among the crowd itself, and even within the ranks of the religious authorities (Jn 7:12–13,31–32,40–49). While some believe that Jesus is a prophet, or even the Messiah, most reject him. The final episode (Jn 7:45–49) encapsulates the theme of belief and rejection running throughout the whole chapter: The rulers condemn the people who believe for being deceived and ignorant of the law. Yet, ironically, one of their own issues a challenge to give Jesus a fair trial before passing judgment (Jn 7:50–51). The other Pharisees respond to Nicodemus, whom we've already met (cf. Jn 3:1–21), "Surely you are not also from Galilee, are you? Search and you will see that no prophet is to arise from Galilee" (Jn 7:52). Opinions about the origin of the Messiah are the root of the controversy.

The Origin of the Messiah (Jn 7:25–36, 40–43)

Two different views about the Messiah's coming are expressed in John 7. One position is summarized in John 7:27, " . . . when the

Messiah comes, no one will know where he is from." According to this eschatological perspective, the Messiah would remain "hidden" until, suddenly, at the right moment, Elijah would reveal him to the world. Along these lines, a few Jewish apocalyptic sects further believed that the Messiah would actually descend from heaven (cf. Dan 7:13; 1 En 48:2,6 and 4 Ezr 13, esp. vv. 51–52).

The second perspective on the Messiah's origins is reflected in the question of the crowd in John 7:42: "Has not the Scripture said that the Messiah is descended from David and comes from Bethlehem, the village where David lived?" The Scripture referred to is Micah 5:2. Matthew 2:5–6 and several rabbinic targums also interpret Micah 5:2 in this way.

On the surface, Jesus meets neither messianic expectation of the people. As far as they can see, Jesus is not "hidden." They've known of him and his place of origin for years. What is more, they know he's from Galilee, not Bethlehem. Since John does not correct the misunderstanding of Galilean origins, scholars have debated whether the fourth evangelist himself even knew of Jesus' actual birthplace. It's most likely that he was aware of the tradition, but to emphasize Bethlehem would have detracted from his point.

John again uses misunderstandings to communicate to his readers at a deeper level. Jesus has a spiritual origin to which most are oblivious. The note sounded several times in preceding chapters of the Gospel is repeated: Jesus has been sent by God (Jn 7:16–18, 28–29, 33). Once he has revealed God's truth, he will return to his heavenly home (Jn 7:33–36). As in John 1:29–51 and 3:13–15, this imagery is used to describe and validate Jesus as the Messiah.

People have read the evidence in a superficial manner and even then they were mistaken. Jesus actually meets all the messianic requirements: his ultimate place of origin remains hidden; he has descended from heaven and been revealed by the prophet like Elijah, John the Baptist; finally, his natural birthplace was Bethlehem. Jesus truly is the Messiah, as those with the Spirit will discern.

Glorification and the Spirit (Jn 7:37–39)

The proclamation of Jesus in John 7:37–39 cannot be fully appreciated apart from its setting on "the great day" of the Feast of Booths. The eighth day of the feast was technically the last, but it was a quiet day of rest on the Sabbath. More likely, Jesus spoke out on the day before. The "great day" was the seventh day, when the ceremonies were concluded with heightened fanfare. Instead of marching around the altar with the water once, as in previous days, on the great day the priests would circle seven times.

Imagine, in this setting, Jesus proclaiming:

Let anyone who is thirsty come to me, and let the one who believes in me drink. As the Scripture has said, "Out of [his] heart shall flow rivers of living water" (Jn 7:37b–38).

The word order and lack of punctuation in the Greek make the exact meaning of this declaration unclear. Is the believer only being invited to drink or is the believer a source of living waters? Given the sense of verse 39 following, most modern exegetes conclude that Jesus alone is the source of "living water." Further, the mission of the believer to others is not developed elsewhere in the chapter. In either reading, however, the main point is clear: the living water ultimately comes from Christ.

Another problem exists with this passage. It is not clear which Scripture is being "quoted" since there is no Old Testament passage that exactly corresponds to the reference in John 7:38. A number have been suggested, the most promising among them being Psalm 78:15–16; 105:40–41; Proverbs 18:4; Zechariah 14:8; Ezekiel 47:1–11; and Isaiah 58:11. Of these, Zechariah 14:8 is perhaps the closest parallel: "On that day living waters shall flow out from Jerusalem . . ."

Due to the agricultural background of the feast, the rite of drawing water represented a prayer for rain in the upcoming growing season. Furthermore, during the ceremony, allusions were made to the provision of water through the rock during the Exodus. Jesus' words may be interpreted, in part, in light of these backgrounds. He provides the water needed for new life to start and he has come to provide life-saving water in the new Exodus. However, there is additional significance to his words, as the evangelist explains in John 7:39.

"Living waters" represent the Spirit. In chapter 4 of this book we have already discussed how "living water" can represent God's revelation as it relates to both the person of Jesus and the Holy Spirit. Here in John 7 we again see the intimate relation between Jesus and the Spirit. Jesus has come to give the Spirit (cf. Jn 1:33), but he cannot do so until he is glorified.

Notably, the hour of Jesus' glorification and the giving of the Spirit are foreshadowed while plans are being made for Jesus' arrest and execution. After his death and resurrection he does give the Spirit (Jn 20:22). This observation leads to the ironic conclusion that the crucifixion marks the glorification of Jesus. Among a people who believed that the Spirit had been withdrawn until the dawning of the messianic era, John makes bold messianic claims for Jesus.

Conclusion

The religious leaders who were awaiting the coming of the Messiah and the full bestowal of the Spirit of God did not accept these very things when they came. In fact, by their unbelief they will, unknowingly, facilitate God's saving plan. They will, in God's time, crucify Jesus. This time is unmistakably and repeatedly foreshadowed in John 7.

The evangelist does more than describe the rejection of Jesus; he prescribes the true verdict regarding him. Within this chapter, we have seen how Jesus meets all messianic requirements even if others do not recognize it. What is more, he fulfills all the hopes embodied in the water-drawing ceremony of the Feast of Booths. He is the source of water that brings life. Is Jesus the Messiah? Does he provide "living water"? The reader must choose which judgment is right.

Before final judgment is passed, however, the next chapter of the Gospel must be considered. Again, a ritual of the feast forms the backdrop for christological truths. The great lamps of the evenings are no comparison to Jesus, the light of the world.

STUDY QUESTIONS

1. List the various dissenting voices you can hear in John 7. When John speaks of "the Jews," to which specific group is he referring?

2. Evaluate the attitude of Jesus' brothers regarding him and his ministry. In comparison, how did Jesus' self-understanding dictate his actions?

3. List all the references in John 7 to Jesus' arrest, crucifixion, and glorification.

4. Describe all the criticisms made of Jesus in John 7. How does the evangelist counter them?

5. What two views of the origins of the Messiah are offered in John 7? How did the people evaluate Jesus in light of each of these views? How does the evangelist?

6. What are the three main rituals associated with the Feast of Booths?

7. How does John build upon the Jewish appreciation of the water-drawing ceremony to teach about Jesus?

8. What are two possible ways of interpreting John 7:38? Which interpretation would you choose? Justify your choice in light of the context and possible Old Testament quotations.

Chapter 8

CONFRONTATIONS:
THE REVEALING LIGHT
(John 8–9)

Introduction

The confrontation at the Feast of Booths continues in John 8 and 9. Many of the same themes found in John 7 are developed further. Questions about the identity, authority, origin, and destination of Jesus persist and divisions among the people widen. More come to believe in Jesus while others strengthen their resolve to kill him.

On the other hand, there are noticeable shifts in the imagery used to communicate these basic themes. Dualisms abound: above and below; truth and lies; life and death; knowledge and ignorance; freedom and slavery—these are all used to create a stark contrast between light and darkness.

Instead of speaking of "living water," Jesus now proclaims: "I am the light of the world" (Jn 8:12; 9:5). This second of the seven "I am" sayings compares Jesus with the spectacular torches lit during the evenings of the Feast of Booths. He alone illuminates the world, providing guidance for some, exposure and condemnation for others.

Rather than asking if Jesus is the Messiah, the dialogue in John 8 reveals the relationship between Father and Son. The discussion of fatherhood forces a comparison in which Jesus supersedes even Abraham. The sixth sign of the Gospel, found in John 9, dramatizes the effect of the light on the world. Jesus makes a blind man see. Not only he, but all witnesses, must choose between walking in light or darkness.

JOHN 8:1–11—THE WOMAN CAUGHT IN ADULTERY

Although the story of the woman taken in adultery shares certain affinities to the Johannine presentation of Christ and his opponents, on textual grounds it is virtually certain that this section was not original to the Gospel of John. Therefore, we will not study it in connection with the rest of John 8.

Even though the textual evidence excludes this section from the Gospel of John in its original form, most scholars are agreed that it is a very early tradition and it accurately represents the spirit of Jesus' teaching.

Adultery, the act of sexual intercourse between a married woman and another man, was punishable by stoning according to the Torah (cf. Lev 20:10, Deut 22:21). By questioning Jesus, the woman's accusers are trying to trap him. Will he deny the Mosaic law outright?

While everyone waits for Jesus to answer, he writes on the ground. Whatever he wrote, it was enough to disperse the elders who were condemning the woman. Since the witnesses to the offense were to be the first to execute punishment (Deut 13:9; 17:7), the case was withdrawn. Jesus himself does not condemn her. Instead, he forgives her and then directs her to sin no more.

The narrative has a powerful message: Christ has not come to condemn but to forgive and transform lives. Strict adherence to a written code, quick condemnation, and discrimination against women were not part of his message. The preservation of this passage shows that the early church embraced the attitude of Jesus.

A Father and His Family (Jn 8:12–59)

Again Jesus spoke to them, saying "I am the light of the world. Whoever follows me will never walk in darkness but will have the light of life" (Jn 8:12).

The significance of "the light of the world" merits a full discussion later. For the moment, however, we note that this pronouncement provokes another legal debate between Jesus and his critics. The Pharisees argue that his testimony is inadmissible. As previously discussed in connection with John 5:31, the statements of at least two witnesses were required to sustain a case in Jewish courts. Further, according to the Mishnah, testimony on one's own behalf was unacceptable (cf. Ketub. 2:9).

Jesus counters that he is not alone; his Father also testifies on his behalf. Even his self-testimony is valid because his origin and mission make his testimony the same as that of his Father (Jn 8:14–18). Such talk of the Father who sent Jesus to testify puzzles the Pharisees. Who is his Father? Where did Jesus come from and where is he going?

The Pharisees cannot comprehend Jesus because his words come "from above" and they are "from below" (Jn 8:23). The two worlds are clear opposites. From one radiates light, knowledge, truth, belief, and life. In the other, there is nothing but darkness, ignorance, lies, sin, and death. The phrase "dying in your sins," found nowhere else in John, is used three times (Jn 8:21,24,24) to stress the bleak state of those who do not believe in Jesus.

It is not only unbelievers whose death is forecast. When Jesus speaks of his departure, the Jews wonder, "Is he going to kill himself?" Their ironic question is an unwitting prophecy. Of course Jesus is not contemplating suicide, as they may have thought. Still, he is consciously moving toward his crucifixion, using the very ones who oppose him to fulfill God's plan of salvation (Jn 8:20,37,40,59). Jesus tells the Jews that when they have "lifted up" the Son of Man, they will finally realize that, as "I am," he is to be identified with God the Father (Jn 8:28-29). Johannine double-meaning is used again: "lifting up" on the cross is also to be understood as "being exalted" (cf. also Jn 3:13–15).

Most of his hearers neither understand nor accept Jesus' words and will consequently be judged by him (Jn 8:25–26). However, it's not all bad news. The evangelist reports that some of "the Jews" began to believe in him (Jn 8:30–31). Jesus exhorts these potential disciples to "continue" in his word, come to know the truth, and be set free.

A problem arises with the response to Jesus in verse 33: some criticize Jesus for insinuating that they need to be freed from anyone. Either the new believers have sudden second thoughts or, more likely, other Jewish hearers are now raising objections. It is doubtful that the Jews who had just expressed faith in Jesus could be the same ones Jesus immediately describes as being murderous, having no place for his word (Jn 8:37,40,43).

Rabbis held that all Israelites were all sons of kings because they were descendants of Abraham, Isaac, and Jacob (Shabbath, 128a). Even when they were politically oppressed, they always maintained the freedom to worship the God of their forefathers. From their perspective, Israelites had never been religious slaves to anyone.

Jesus contradicts them (Jn 8:34–38). Even a descendant of Abraham may be enslaved at the spiritual level. By seeking to kill Jesus, these Jews show that they no longer occupy a place in God's household as sons. True sons would listen to the words from their Father that Jesus speaks. Jesus' accusers are not free; they are not sons. They are slaves to the sin in their lives.

Nonplussed, the Jews can only repeat, "Abraham is our father" (Jn 8:39), but Jesus casts doubt even on that. Children follow their father's example and his adversaries are behaving like the devil, not Abraham. The devil is a murderer who cannot stand in the presence of truth. Consequently his children cannot accept Jesus' word and want to kill the one who speaks the truth from God.

The Jews turn Jesus' words back on him. *He* is illegitimate and demonic, not they (Jn 8:48, cf. also 41 and 52). Calling him a Samaritan implied that he was a deranged heretic outside of the true descendancy of Abraham. Jesus counters by saying he is not seeking the honor they refuse to give him; God will glorify him (Jn 8:50,54). What is more, those who know Jesus and keep his word, as Jesus knows God and keeps God's word, "will never see death" (Jn 8:51).

Because Jesus has promised to overcome death, he is asked, "Are you greater than our father Abraham, who died?" Though meant to underscore the absurdity of Jesus' claims, the rhetorical question ironically expresses truth. Yes, Jesus is greater than Abraham and, what is more, Abraham has gladly witnessed the saving work of Jesus (Jn 8:56). This prompts another rhetorical question: how could Jesus, still in the prime of his life, be old enough to have seen Abraham (Jn 8:57)? Again Jesus answers unexpectedly, saying, " . . . before Abraham was, I am" (Jn 8:58). Perhaps the most striking "I am" statement in the Gospel, this announcement unequivocally identifies Jesus with the pre-existent God (cf. Jn 1:1).

Everyone understands Jesus now, but they don't accept his position. In angry reaction to his apparent blasphemy, the Jews prepare to stone him without delay. However, his hour has still not come and Jesus leaves the temple, escaping an untimely death at the hands of the mob.

Walking in Light and Darkness (Jn 9:1–41)

The exit from the temple is not the end of John's presentation of Jesus at the Feast in Jerusalem. John 8 began with Jesus' words in the temple court: "I am the light of the world" (Jn 8:12); now the saying is echoed as Jesus performs a sign that develops the theme of light further (Jn 9:5).

The end of every day of the feast was marked by an elaborate, festive lamp-lighting ceremony in the court of the women. Four huge lamps were lit, each containing approximately 65 liters of oil, with wicks made from discarded priestly robes. The Mishnah reports, "There was no courtyard in Jerusalem which was not made bright by the light" (Sukka 5:3b). With torches in their hands, people danced and sang in festal joy throughout the night, celebrating God's presence with them in the pillar of fire during the nights of the Exodus. It is with these associations, in this very court, that Jesus stood and first proclaimed, "I am the light of the world. He who follows me will not walk in darkness, but will have the light of life" (Jn 8:12). As he heals the blind man, he repeats, "As long as I am in the world, I am the light of the world" (Jn 9:5).

We can well imagine the impact of such a statement at the feast. Comparisons are being made: more than the great lamps and many torches which light up the Jerusalem night, and more than a pillar of fire for some Hebrew wanderers, Jesus alone illuminates on an eternal, cosmic scale. He shines the light of life upon all humanity, whether Jewish or Gentile, to lead the way in a greater, second Exodus.

Light is a natural symbol for God's revelation and the language would have been easily understood by readers of all backgrounds. The paramount, universal, and unique claim of Jesus to be *the* light of the world would not be overlooked, especially with the employment of the "I am" formula in John 8:12.

The message that Jesus is the light of the world is conveyed not only in the saying; it is also enacted in a series of seven scenes in John 9 (see box). In the first scene, he heals a blind man (Jn 9:1–7). A series of six testimonies follow: neighbors question the man (Jn 9:8–12); the Pharisees also interrogate him (Jn 9:13–17); they then question his parents (Jn 9:18–23); the man is again summoned (Jn 9:24–34); he has a reunion with Jesus during which he comes to faith (Jn 9:35–38); and finally the division between the spiritually blind and sighted is made (Jn 9:39–41).

That the healed man was described as blind "from birth" is significant. The extent of his affliction and Jesus' healing power is thus established. In addition, though, it gives some background to the discussion about sin and suffering which immediately follows. When a child was born with a sickness, the traditional retributive link between sin and suffering was challenged. Rabbis would often turn to Exodus 20:5 for a solution: the children were being punished for the sins of their fathers. Still others, building on the description of Jacob

A SERIES OF INTERROGATIONS

The message that Jesus is the light of the world is enacted in a series of seven interrogations in John 9:

1. John 9:1–7—Jesus and the blind man.

   Question (from the disciples): "Rabbi, who sinned, this man or his parents, that he was born blind?"
   Answer (from Jesus): "Neither this man nor his parents sinned; he was born blind so that God's works might be revealed in him."
   Jesus then heals the blind man.

2. John 9:8–12—The neighbors of the man

   Questions (from the neighbors): "Is this not the man who used to sit and beg? . . . How were your eyes opened? . . Where is he [Jesus]?"
   Answers (from the healed man): "I am the man . . . the man called Jesus made mud, spread it on my eyes . . . told me to wash . . . and I received my sight."

3. John 9:13–17—The Pharisees and the man

   Questions (from the Pharisees): "How did you receive your sight? . . . How can a man who is a sinner perform such signs? . . . What do you say about him?"
   Answers (from the man): "He put mud on my eyes. Then I washed, and now I see . . . He is a prophet."

4. John 9:18–23—The Pharisees and the parents of the man

   Questions (from the Pharisees): "Is this your son, who you say was born blind? How then does he now see?"
   Answers (from the parents): "We know this is our son, and that he was born blind; but we do not know how it is that now he sees, nor do we know who opened his eyes. Ask him; he is of age."

5. John 9:24–34—The Pharisees and the man, again

   Questions (from the Pharisees): "What did he do to you? How did he open your eyes?"
   Answers (from the man): "I have told you already, and you would not listen . . . Do you also want to become his disciples?"
   Exasperated, the Pharisees drive him out, saying, "You were born entirely in sin, and are you trying to teach us?"

6. John 9:35–39—Jesus and the blind man, again

   Question (from Jesus): "Do you believe in the Son of Man?"
   Answer (from the man): "Lord, I believe."

7. John 9:40–41—The Pharisees and Jesus

   Question (from the Pharisees): "Surely we are not blind, are we?"
   Answer (from Jesus): "If you were blind, you would not have sin. But now that you say 'We see,' your sin remains."

and Esau in Rebecca's womb (Gen 25:22, cf. Gen. Rab. 63:69c), taught that babies could sin in their mothers' wombs.

Jesus did not enter into the debate concerning the relationship between sin and suffering. Rather, he maintained that this man's blindness was not the result of anyone's sin; it was intended to lead to the glorification of God by the revelation of his works (cf. Jn 11:4). On the other hand, we have already seen how Jesus did link sin and suffering in one particular instance: the healing of the paralytic (Jn 5:14).

Perhaps adapting a proverb, Jesus speaks about working during the day instead of the night: "We must work the works of him who sent me while it is day; night is coming when no one can work" (Jn 9:4). This statement and subsequent actions make two important points. First, giving sight is God's work. Second, others besides Jesus carry out the work of God.

According to the Old Testament, the dawning of the messianic age would be confirmed by the giving of sight to the blind (Isa 29:18; 35:5; 42:7) and so this act of Jesus is a messianic announcement. As in Mark 7:33 and 8:12, Jesus uses saliva to heal. Interestingly, this practice was associated with magic in ancient times, compelling rabbis to prohibit its therapeutic use (Tos. Sanh. 12:10). Possibly to avoid the charge that Jesus was a magician, Matthew and Luke have omitted these particular miracles. From the second century on, the Christian church has interpreted Jesus' command to wash (Jn 9:7,11,15) sacramentally as a reference to baptism, although the evidence in John itself for such an understanding is slight.

Jesus includes his disciples in God's work by saying, "*We* must do the work of him who has sent me" (Jn 9:4). The shared task extends beyond the immediate circle of Jesus' first disciples to those who believe after his crucifixion (Jn 14:12). No doubt the readers of the Gospel are being urged to continue the work of Jesus. Some interpreters have suggested that the play on words in John 9:7 contributes to the commissioning. The man was *sent* to the Pool of Siloam and the evangelist alludes to the similarity between the name "Siloam" and the verb "to send." As Jesus has been sent (Jn 9:4), he sends others (cf. also Jn 20:21).

The man returns healed. As the news spreads, divisions arise immediately. Some believe that the blind man they've known for some time has received his sight, others do not think he's the same person (Jn 9:9). This will not be the last time in this chapter that a division among the people is recorded (Jn 9:16, 39). The light Jesus sheds will be welcomed by some and avoided by others.

A motif of gradual recognition is used again by the evangelist. Just as the healed paralytic could not at first tell where Jesus had gone (Jn 5:13), the man who could now see did not know where his healer was (Jn 9:12). In both cases Jesus returns to offer further illumination, leading the reader through the process of coming to faith.

Again Jesus has healed on the Sabbath, to the consternation of the Pharisees (9:14,16; cf. 5:9–10). They claim, "This man is not from God, for he does not observe the sabbath" (Jn 9:16). As far as they are concerned, he is a sinner (Jn 9:16,24). In their position as religious authorities, the interrogators presume a knowledge of God and his ways, which, in fact, they do not have. To the end of this narrative, their attitude does not change. They say they see, but they remain blind in their sin (Jn 9:39–41).

Compare the posture of the Pharisees with others in this drama. The healed man and his parents are without pretense. They do not claim to deserve favor from God and they admit they do not understand Jesus' ways. They do have one irrefutable testimony: the man was blind and, because of Jesus, he can now see. The salvation Jesus offers is not conditional on religious presumption.

Tension between those who support Jesus and those who oppose him is growing. The reaction of the blind man's parents during their questioning reveals an important development in synagogue life. The parents are afraid of excommunication because of their association with Jesus, who was now deemed a false Messiah (Jn 9:22; cf. also Jn 7:13). Interpreters see here a secondary reference to the experience of the Johannine community. The Johannine Christians have been banned from the synagogue and experienced the full wrath of its rulers (see also Jn 16:1–4). The Johannine polemic against "the Jews" must be read in this context.

With exemplary courage, the blind man who was healed stands up to the grilling and insists that Jesus has come from God. In anger the authorities call him a sinner like Jesus and drive him out. The climax of the drama follows (Jn 9:35–38). Jesus hears that the man has been expelled and searches him out. He reveals himself as the "Son of Man." In turn, the man confesses faith in him and gives him the honor due God. The transition from physical blindness to sight was only a precursor to this ultimate journey from spiritual blindness to the light of belief. It is John's hope that his readers will follow in the steps of the healed blind man against increasingly entrenched opposition and blind unbelief.

Conclusion

Jesus embodies another ritual in the Feast of Booths. The great lamps and torches at the temple in the evening dim beside Jesus, the light of the world. As the light, he reveals. John 8, in particular, deals with the way in which Jesus reveals the Father. John 9 shows the world's response. Once exposed to the light, all must decide either to walk in illumination or darkness.

As much is revealed about the Son as the Father when Jesus shines his light. Together, they are the only hope for freedom and life. Descendancy from Abraham, in spite of the views of his Jewish contemporaries, offers no guarantee of deliverance. Although both Jesus and his critics maintain that God is their Father, Jesus insists that anyone who cannot believe in him does not have the same heavenly Father. Because his adversaries deceive the people and plot his death, their real father must be the devil, a murderer and the father of lies. Jesus finally moves beyond the Pharisaic threshold when he invokes the name of God in self-identification. They try to kill him, but they will not succeed, yet.

Enacting his function as light of the world, Jesus enlightens a blind man's life. In answer to the question "Who has sinned?" one cannot reply "the blind man" or "Jesus." The closed-minded people who refuse to believe Jesus are culpable. The light gradually ignites for some in John 8–9, but, tragically, it flickers out in the hearts of others. Those who do not believe will die in sin, but not before they participate in Jesus' death. Fortunately for those who believe, his death will only be temporary.

STUDY QUESTIONS

1. How does the statement "I am the light of the world" relate to the setting in which it was spoken? What are some of its implications in this context?

2. The Pharisees argue that Jesus' claim to be the light of the world cannot be sustained. What reasons do they give? How does Jesus counter their arguments?

3. Jesus compares what is "from above" with what is "from below." What are some other corresponding dualisms mentioned? What do these comparisons tell you about life with and without Christ?

4. Did everyone in John 8 oppose Jesus? Can the people in John 8:30–32 be the same ones he speaks to in verses 33–38? How can you fit these descriptions together?

5. True sonship is at issue in John 8. How are the Jews' family lines challenged by Jesus? How are Jesus' challenged? Who are the three fathers mentioned in this chapter?

6. Why is it important to note that the man in John 9 was blind "from birth"? Compare and contrast the healing of the paralytic in John 5 with the blind man here in John 9: look at the condition of the two men, the actions of Jesus, and the response of the onlookers.

7. Contrast the religious attitude of the Pharisees with that of the blind man. What relationship does religious knowledge have to saving belief?

8. What was the response of the synagogue to Jewish Christians? How is it dramatized in the experience of the healed man? What indications in the Gospel are there that this is also the experience of the Johannine community?

9. Trace the transition from light to darkness in the experience of the blind man. When was the journey completed?

Chapter 9

LAYING DOWN HIS LIFE: FINAL FORESHADOWING
(John 10–11)

Introduction

A new emphasis on the intimacy between Jesus and his followers surfaces with John 10, albeit still in a context of opposition. In the next three chapters of the Gospel, word and deed together proclaim that the forthcoming death of Jesus is not so much a tragedy as a victory. Jesus voluntarily enters into death and has the power to overcome its hold on those whom he loves.

Chapter 10 contains perhaps the only parable found in John. We meet a good shepherd who protects his sheep from intruders and impostors. By two more "I am" sayings embedded in the Johannine parable, Jesus lays exclusive claim to open the way for the salvation of his followers. The personal relationship he enjoys with everyone whom he shepherds is founded on his own bond with the Father.

The raising of Lazarus (Jn 11) not only demonstrates the love and power of the good shepherd; it foreshadows his own death and resurrection. This seventh sign also precipitates the crucifixion of the one who says "I am the resurrection and the life."

The Good Shepherd (Jn 10:1–42)

While is it customary to call the "figure of speech" (Jn 10:6) in this chapter a parable, it does not have the same traits as the Synoptic parables. Neither is it strictly an allegory, since the metaphorical language is not consistent enough. Rather, Jesus loosely strings together aspects of sheep farming—a pen, a gate, sheep, a shepherd, a gatekeeper, a hired hand, strangers, thieves, bandits, and a wolf—to make several points.

His first point concerns access to the sheepfold.

The first of the two "I am" sayings, "I am the gate" (Jn 10:7,9), presents Jesus as the way to salvation *and* the guard from outside threats. Commentators tend to focus upon one or the other, but both functions of the gate appear in the narrative.

John 10:9 could not be more explicitly soteriological: "I am the gate. Whoever enters by me will be saved, and will come in and go out and find pasture." Psalm 118, which was interpreted messianically by the early church, serves as a background: "This is the gate of the Lord; the righteous shall enter through it" (Ps 118:20). Jesus is the gate for the sheep to find salvation.

Jesus as the gate also restricts access *to* the sheep. In preparation for Jesus' claim to be the good shepherd, verses 1–3 stress that only the rightful shepherd enters freely by way of the gate; the "thief and bandit" can enter only surreptitiously. Again verse 8, separating the two "I am the gate" sayings, mentions that "thieves and bandits" do not have access.

Most commentators treat the reference to robbers as a thinly veiled criticism of the Pharisees and Sadducees. Others see an allusion to Moses and the prophets. A few scholars suggest that the Gospel is denouncing either Gnostic redeemers, the Qumran Teacher of Righteousness, contemporary insurrectionists, or self-proclaimed false messiahs. Although the context and Old Testament background suggest that Israel's religious establishment are the culprits here, there is no need to be specific. Compared to Jesus, *everyone* else who tries to lead the sheep is a thief or bandit. The privilege of entrance is exclusive. In guarding the sheep, Jesus allows legitimate entrance to no others.

The gate and the shepherd could be literally the same since the shepherd would often sleep across the opening of the sheepfold as a human "gate." The description of the shepherd as "laying down his life for the sheep" (Jn 10:11, 15, 17–18) may be significant in this respect. On the other hand, an actual gate, and a gatekeeper distinguished from the shepherd, also appear in John 10:3.

In contrast to all others who would claim to be shepherds of the flock of God, only Jesus can say "I am the good shepherd" (Jn 10:11,14). The two words qualifying "shepherd" are noteworthy. Jesus is *the good* shepherd: no other shepherd is good.

Ezekiel 34 forms a fitting backdrop for Jesus' comparison of himself with other so-called "shepherds of Israel." These shepherds of Israel are condemned in Ezekiel 34 for abandoning their responsibility to care for the sheep. Instead, they care for themselves, much like the hired hands of John 10:12–14. Those who were to feed and heal the sheep slaughtered and ate them (Ez 34:3–4), like the thief who only comes to steal, kill, and destroy (Jn 10:10). Forsaken, the scattered flock became food for wild animals (cf. Ez 34:5–6; Jn 10:12).

God's judgment is decisive. The shepherds will be removed and God himself will tend the sheep (Ez 34:15). He will search for the lost sheep and gather them together into one flock to enjoy again good pasture (Ez 34:11–16). He will place over the flock one shepherd, the Davidic Messiah. The prophecy ends with the words of the Lord: "They shall know that I, the Lord their God, am with them, and that they, the house of Israel, are my people, says the Lord God. You are my sheep, the sheep of my pasture, and I am your God, says the Lord God" (Ez 34:30–31).

The remarkable parallels between Ezekiel and John 10 herald the fulfillment of the prophecy in Jesus. He tells the religious authorities that he has come to tend the sheep they have neglected and mistreated. He will find the lost sheep and gather the scattered flock, "so there will be one flock, one shepherd" (Jn 10:16). He will protect them from thieves, self-serving undershepherds, and wild animals. They can "come in and go out and find pasture" (Jn 10:9). The sheep will run from strangers and follow only him, for, as Jesus says, "I know my own and my own know me" (Jn 10:14).

Unlike a hired hand who abandons the flock to attacking wolves, Jesus willingly dies for his sheep. While the accidental death of a shepherd in defense of the sheep is conceivable, voluntary death is a somewhat unexpected and dominant theme. It pushes the definition of what makes a "good" shepherd beyond generally held criteria. Jesus says, "No one takes it [life] from me, but I lay it down of my own accord" (Jn 10:18). More surprising, Jesus not only has the power to lay down his life, he has the power to take it up again (Jn 10:17–18). Jesus is no victim and his death is no accident; his resurrection is part of the saving plan of God.

Jesus must die and rise again so that his sheep can share in his victory over death. He has come to provide abundant, eternal life (Jn 10:10,28). Since the eternal quality originates only from God, the eternal life he gives must be linked to God. It is the life that has been going on before time and continues on beyond time. It is full and never-ending life as God intended.

Eternal life is secure. No danger can provoke the shepherd to abandon his sheep; they will never be left to die (Jn 10:28-30). The good shepherd can make this promise because he is acting for the Father, who is greater than all. Note the clear parallel between the action of Jesus and the action of his Father in these verses. Speaking of his sheep, Jesus says, " . . . No one will snatch them out of *my hand*" (Jn 10:28). He immediately goes on to say, " . . . no one can snatch them out of *my Father's hand*" (Jn 10:29–30). The unity between the Father and Son is thorough and functional: Jesus is God working in the world. He has God's authority and ability to give eternal life.

The sheep are a gift from the Father to his Son (Jn 10:29). The Father loves his Son (Jn 10:17) and has commanded him to lay down and take up his life (Jn 10:18). The Father has dedicated the Son to this mission (Jn 10:36) and Jesus responds in obedience. They share one will and one purpose. As Jesus says, " . . . the Father is in me and I am in the Father" (Jn 10:38).

The Father-Son relationship is woven into the good shepherd metaphor not only to develop the themes of unity and obedience, but also to provide the foundation for the intimate connection between Jesus and his followers. He knows his sheep and they know him, just as the Father and Son know each other (Jn 10:14–15). He calls them by name and they follow his voice alone (Jn 10:3-5,16,27).

To this day in the Middle East, the shepherd walks ahead of the flock, calling the sheep on with his voice, rather than driving them from behind as in Western culture. The picture, then, is an appropriate illustration of the relationship between master and disciple. For the sheep to experience the life the good shepherd provides, they must listen for his voice and follow him. For Jesus' sheep, following involves listening, understanding, believing, and depending upon Jesus.

Not all sheep belong to the flock of Jesus. Among these "outsiders" are some Jewish leaders; they do not recognize the voice of Jesus and trust in him (Jn 10:6, 25–26). However, there are sheep not part of the present flock who will respond to Jesus' voice. He says, "I have other sheep that do not belong to this fold. I must bring them also, and they will listen to my voice. So there will be one flock, one shepherd" (Jn 10:16).

Who are these other sheep? Fanciful theories abound. This one verse has been abused by many religious movements through the ages to claim the blessing of Jesus on their eccentricities. Of course, when the words were first spoken none of these explanations would make sense. Almost certainly, the "other sheep" to whom Jesus referred were Gentiles who would come to faith in him, joining Jewish believers in the Christian flock (cf. also Jn 11:52).

Years later, however, the first readers might have understood the reference to these "other sheep" as non-Johannine Christians who are nonetheless being commended to them by the evangelist or editor. The Johannine community eventually did merge with other Christians into "one flock" with "one shepherd," perhaps due, in part, to statements such as John 10:16. Jesus came to unite all believers with God and one another.

The Johannine parable of the good shepherd presents Jesus as both the way to, and source of, abundant eternal life. Jesus announces that he alone has rightful charge over the sheep and he will lay down his life to protect them from interlopers. As God's Son, he is God's agent among humanity.

Predictably, the Jews cannot accept Jesus' claims to be God's Son. Jesus defends himself with a method familiar to his rabbinic accusers: he quotes Psalm 82:6 as an example where men are called "gods." If Scripture can call unjust mortals "gods," surely he can call himself God's Son. His argument was rejected. One more time the Jews try to put him to death and one more time he escapes (Jn 10:31, 39). Outside Judea, more people come to believe in him (Jn 10:40–42).

The Resurrection and the Life (Jn 11:1–57)

The discourse of chapter 10 and the sign of chapter 11 share the principal theme of death and resurrection. The discourse teaches us that Jesus, as the good shepherd, has the power to lay down his life and raise it up again at will. The sign concretizes the parable in *real* relationships with *real* people.

Jesus uses his power to raise the dead man Lazarus and by that very action accelerates plans for his own death and consequent resurrection. Also, as only the good shepherd can, Jesus harbors deep feelings for his sheep. This is an account of a death in a family Jesus loved.

In John 11, we are introduced to three close friends of Jesus: Mary, Martha, and Lazarus. Mary and Martha appear also in Luke 10:38–42, where we are told more of their individual personalities and respective relationships with Jesus. As well, John tells us in retrospect that Mary was the one who anointed Jesus with perfume (Jn 11:2, cf. 12:1–8).

Lazarus is seen only in John 11 and 12, although the same name is used in a parable (Lk 16:19–31). When he becomes seriously sick, his sisters send word to Jesus: "Lord, the one whom you love is ill" (Jn 11:3). Because Lazarus is described as the one whom Jesus loved in verses 3, 5 and 36, a few interpreters have speculated that Lazarus was the "Beloved Disciple" behind the Fourth Gospel. As intriguing as the theory may be, the evidence is inconclusive.

Responding to the news of Lazarus' condition, Jesus assures the women that it is not the Father's purpose that Lazarus die but that God's glory might be seen in his Son. Still, Lazarus does die, but his death does not close the story.

Tension builds as Jesus deliberately waits before making the trip to Lazarus' home in Bethany (Jn 11:6, cf. also 11:15). While he waits, Lazarus dies. By delaying, Jesus actually lays down a life. He does not avoid death, he confronts it in its finality to conquer it. The glory of which Jesus speaks (Jn 11:4) is ultimately seen through death.

When Jesus finally does go to Bethany, his disciples counsel against it because of the hostile religious authorities. Jesus responds enigmatically: "Are there not twelve hours of daylight? Those who walk during the day do not stumble, because they see the light of this world. But those who walk at night stumble, because the light is not in them" (Jn 11:9–10). As with many of Jesus' statements, this can be read on more than one level. On the surface, Jesus is saying that he must carry out his ministry while he still has the opportunity; his time is limited. On a deeper level, he is speaking of himself as the light. Those who walk with the light of Jesus' revelation will be led through life without stumbling; those who choose not to walk with Jesus will stumble.

Another double meaning occurs in John 11:11–14: the disciples are told that Lazarus has "fallen asleep" and Jesus must go to wake him. Although sleep was a common euphemism for death, the disciples misunderstand. In context, their response is absurd: they reason that if Lazarus is allowed to sleep, he will recover! Their confusion allows Jesus to confirm Lazarus' death and state the purpose behind Jesus' delay (Jn 11:15). The resurrection of Lazarus points to a specific spiritual truth that would not be communicated if Jesus "merely" healed Lazarus before he died. Now it is time to visit the grave of Lazarus.

At this point we hear from a disciple who speaks only in the Gospel of John. Whenever Thomas speaks (Jn 11:16; 14:5 and 20:24–29) it is difficult to discern whether his frank comments are pessimistic or sincere, but always they present a call to faith. Thomas tells his fellow disciples that they should go with Jesus, "that we may die with him" (Jn 11:16). The words express more than Thomas could realize: at the spiritual level, every believer must follow Jesus through death to eternal life.

When Jesus arrived, Lazarus had been in the tomb for four days (Jn 11:17). The four days are important because the rabbis taught that the soul remains at the grave site for three days, yearning to return to the body (Gen. Rab. 100:64). Any hope for Lazarus' resuscitation had passed.

Mary and Martha had faith in Jesus' ability to heal, but their hope had given way to regret. Both women told Jesus that if he had come earlier, Lazarus would not have died (Jn 11:21 and 32). In particular, Martha's faith allowed her to accept that all was not over. Martha knows that God will grant Jesus his desires for Lazarus and she knows that, in any event, Lazarus will be raised on the last day (Jn 11:22–25). Still, Jesus is going to give her even more hope.

Speaking to Martha, Jesus utters his fifth "I am" saying: "I am the resurrection and the life; those who believe in me, even though they die, will live, and everyone who lives and believes in me will never die" (Jn 11:25–26).

This saying affirms that Christ's life-giving work affects our life on two levels in two time-frames. In the future, Jesus will bring physical life again, but in the present, Jesus brings eternal life. The fact that he *is* the resurrection and life, and does not merely *offer* resurrection and life, shows that his saving work is totally integrated into his very being and those who believe are uniting with him.

At the tomb, with all the mourners present, Jesus himself is moved (Jn 11:33,35,38). His feelings are not clear, but presumably he was as disturbed as the others at the pain and loss brought on by the destructive powers of death. God grieves with people in the face of death.

At the tomb, Jesus orders the stone to be rolled away, to the horror of the crowd. Jewish burial practice required several steps. First, the corpse, completely wrapped in linen, would be laid down on a stone shelf or table in the tomb to decompose. Then, up to a year later, the mourners would reenter the tomb, gather the bones and deposit them in urns that were then placed in cavities carved in the walls. Several generations would thus share the tomb. At this point, after four days, the body would have begun its decay and it would be both repulsive and ritually impure to open the tomb.

Nevertheless, Jesus reminds Martha of the promise of seeing God's glory and they move the stone. Jesus prays to the Father for the sake of his audience. The wording of John 11:42 suggests that Jesus was always in communication with his Father and his words show *others* that the Son is working in union with the Father.

The miracle is told briefly. Just as the sheep respond to the voice of their good shepherd, Lazarus responds to the call of Jesus and walks out of the tomb. He is released from the grave clothes at Jesus' command. Christ has released humanity from all that binds and oppresses, even the power of death.

The reaction to the resurrection of Lazarus is mixed. On the one hand, many of the Jews believed in Jesus because of what they witnessed (Jn 1:45). On the other hand, when the Pharisees hear of the event, they call a council meeting to decide on how finally to put a stop to Jesus (Jn 11:46–57). The council feared a mass movement to Jesus that would jeopardize not only their position but the nation itself. Opposition to Jesus is now political as well as religious. Jesus was put to death, in part, by the forces of Roman imperialism.

At the meeting, the high priest Caiaphas tells the council: " . . . it is expedient for you to have one man die for the people, than to have the whole nation destroyed." Here John's irony is elevated to the status of prophecy. Jesus will die for salvation of the nation, although Caiaphas did not understand the extent of the salvation Jesus would thereby bring. His death would be redemptive and unifying for all, both Jew and Gentile (Jn 11:52).

Conclusion

Together, chapters 10 and 11 of the Gospel proclaim that Jesus is the Lord over death. Surpassing the devotion of any other shepherd, Jesus loves intimately every one of his sheep. He voluntarily enters death's grasp with the power to overcome its hold on those whom he loves. The dramatic foreshadowing of Jesus' death and resurrection makes the seventh sign a fitting climax to the "Book of Signs" (John 1–12), for it shows that the saving, revealing work of Christ comes through his personal victory over death.

There are now standing orders for Jesus' arrest and so the time has come for Jesus to wind down his public ministry. He will appear in public within the week for his last Passover celebration.

STUDY QUESTIONS

1. What two functions does a gate have? How do these two functions relate to the role of Jesus with respect to the sheep in the fold?

2. What does it mean to say that Jesus is the good shepherd in comparison to the thieves?—the gatekeeper?—the hired hand?

3. Jesus speaks of a shepherd laying down his life for the sheep. What two scenarios in the life of a shepherd are being represented here? In what ways will Jesus' "laying down" parallel and supersede that of an actual shepherd?

4. What do we learn about the relationship between the Son and the Father in John 10? What do we learn about the relationship between the Son and his "sheep"?

5. What indications are there in both John 10 and 11 that Jesus envisaged a ministry to non-Jews?

6. Why did Jesus wait after being told of Lazarus' illness?

7. What are some implications of Jesus' statement "I am the resurrection and the life"?

8. Find examples of both misunderstanding and irony used in John 11 to communicate at a deeper level to the reader.

9. How does the seventh sign function in relation to the discourse of John 10? How does it function in relation to the upcoming death of Jesus?

Chapter 10

LAYING DOWN HIS LIFE:
LEAVING THE PUBLIC EYE
(John 12)

Introduction

The gift of life that Jesus gave to Lazarus is the occasion for both celebration and condemnation. John 12 starts on a high point with a party in honor of Jesus and an exultant procession into Jerusalem. The chapter ends somberly as Jesus withdraws from an unbelieving, hostile public. With the last discourse spoken and the final sign completed, Jesus reminds his hearers that they will be judged according to their response to him. Their understanding of Jesus reveals their understanding of God.

Celebration for the Victorious King (Jn 12:1–19)

Back in Bethany, Jesus' last sign continues to generate excitement among both his friends and enemies. Some hold a dinner for Jesus where a woman anoints him with perfume. Objections about her behavior are raised. Unlike the more general Synoptic parallels (Mt 26:6–13; Mk 14:3–9; Lk 7:36–50), John specifically names three people as he unfolds the theology behind the actions. Lazarus provokes faith and judgment. Mary anoints for coronation and burial. Judas unwittingly unmasks the priorities of good and evil.

Three times in chapter 12, John calls Lazarus "the one whom Jesus raised from the dead" (Jn 12:1,6,17). This distinction draws Lazarus into the arena with Jesus. People now react to him as they do

87

to Jesus: some come to faith through him and others decide he also must die (Jn 12:9–11, 17–19).

During dinner, Lazarus reclines with Jesus. The language describing the intimate picture foreshadows the supper scene in John 13. The same Greek word describes how the Beloved Disciple rested next to Jesus during the last supper (Jn 13:23–25). This may be another subtle way of identifying the Beloved Disciple, but again the evidence is tenuous.

Mary builds another bridge between the meal in Bethany and the last supper. She anoints Jesus' feet and wipes them with her hair; later Jesus will wash the disciples' feet (Jn 13:1–11). Mary's ointment is nard, made from an aromatic herb grown in the Himalayas. Imported in alabaster boxes, the costly perfume scented the couches of kings (Song 1:12), anointed the heads of royalty at coronations, and embalmed corpses. Normally, *feet* were anointed only for burial and so Mary's loving actions were primarily an embalming (Jn 12:7). Nevertheless, we see other allusions to Jesus as the anointed king, the Messiah (cf. esp. Jn 12:12–15). Jesus, the king, will reign by dying.

For his part, Judas inadvertently exposes his motives for betraying Jesus, again pointing toward events at the last supper. He feigns concern about the price of the ointment—about a year's wages—being spent on perfume instead of charity. Jesus responds ambiguously: "Leave her alone. She bought it so that she might keep it for the day of my burial. You always have the poor with you, but you do not always have me" (Jn 12:7–8). The time for Jesus' burial has arrived and he is now prepared. His death, in turn, will minister to all, including the poor.

What began as an intimate gathering soon attracts a crowd wanting to see, not only Jesus, but also the man he raised from the dead. Momentum is gathering as more turn to faith in Jesus, to the consternation of the chief priests. As growing numbers prepare to usher the royal deliverer into Jerusalem, the religious leaders resolve to eliminate the proof of his saving power, Lazarus.

John's account of the entry into the city is shorter than those of the Synoptics. He focuses to show that Jesus fulfills Israel's hope for a king. The cheer of Psalm 118:26 and the waving of palm fronds express nationalistic fervor in the wake of deliverance from oppressors. Jesus is "the king of Israel" (Jn 12:13). This king, however, is not what they expected. Only in retrospect, after Jesus' death and resurrection, did the disciples realize the true nature of Jesus' messianic kingship (Jn 12:16–18).

After battle, a victorious king would normally return on a mighty war horse to receive homage. In contrast, Jesus enters Jerusalem on a lowly donkey in fulfillment of Scripture. The quotation of Zechariah 9:9 in John 12:15 is not exact. Zechariah says "Rejoice greatly . . . " where John reads "Do not be afraid . . . " John is likely merging part of a related passage: Zephaniah 3:16. Zephaniah's announcement of victory has a more universalistic, less nationalistic, scope. John presents the king coming in peace, not war; delivering the world, not just Israel.

Witnessing the crowd praise Jesus, the Pharisees exclaim "the whole world has gone after him!" (Jn 12:19). They have exaggerated in their despair, but their words anticipate the next scene where representatives of other nations come to see Jesus. He is about to leave a message of life and death to all humanity.

Parting Words to the World (Jn 12:20–50)

Jews were not the only ones in Jerusalem during the Passover. Greeks also participated. They were Gentiles attracted to Judaism, though not necessarily full converts. At the temple, they were permitted only into the court of the Gentiles. It was perhaps here that they asked Philip about meeting Jesus.

Why they approached Philip instead of Jesus is unclear. The Greeks may have mistakenly thought he was Greek since he had a Greek name and came from Bethsaida (Jn 12:21). In any case, John develops a missionary pattern: again Philip joins Andrew, and again the two men bring someone to Jesus (cf. Jn 1:43–45 and 6:5–90).

Nothing more is said about the Greek visitors, but their presence is pivotal. The hour has come, and both Jews and Gentiles are present to witness Christ's glorification.

Paradoxically, the hour of glorification begins with death. Jesus invokes a familiar religious symbol of life springing from death: the seed (Jn 12:24). After its burial comes resurrection and multiplication. Jesus, like a kernel of wheat, must be buried to produce a rich harvest. If he does not die, there will be no life for others; he alone will live.

As with their master, disciples also must surrender their life. "Those who love their life lose it, and those who hate their life in this world will keep it for eternal life" (Jn 12:25). Of the five versions of this saying in the New Testament, John's is the most potent (see box). It is the shortest and alone employs the "love/hate" contrast. The hyperbole of loving and hating conveys the sense that no one can ultimately live at all if one clings to one's personal existence rather

---

SELF–SURRENDER IN THE GOSPELS

. . . For those who want to save their life will lose it, and those who lose their life for my sake will find it (Mt 16:25).

. . . For those who want to save their life will lose it and those who lose their life for my sake will save it (Lk 9:24).

. . . For those who want to save their life will lose it, and those who lose their life for my sake, and for the sake of the gospel, will save it (Mk 8:35).

Those who try to make their life secure will lose it, but those who lose their life will keep it (Lk 17:33).

Those who love their life will lose it, and those who hate their life in this world will keep it for eternal life (Jn 12:25).

---

than embracing Jesus. Disciples will serve Jesus by imitating his self-surrender (Jn 12:26). If they follow him in death to self, they also will be with him in resurrection to eternal life.

Of course, people instinctively want to save their lives rather than give them up and as a human being Jesus was no exception. He confesses his struggle with fear and the desire for self-preservation: "Now my soul is troubled. And what should I say—'Father, save me from this hour'? No, it is for this reason that I have come to this hour" (Jn 12:27).

This one brief statement condenses the longer Synoptic descriptions of Jesus' agonizing prayer at Gethsemane when he pleaded with the Father to remove his cup of suffering and death (Mt 26:36–46; Mk 14:32,42; Lk 22:39–46). John does not speak of this despair in his account of the prayer in the garden (Jn 17). In John, the hour of death is glorious and victorious. Still, even if these earlier second thoughts in John are momentary, they are strong. The same word describes his feelings here as his mourning for Lazarus (Jn 11:33) and his anguish at the announcement of betrayal (Jn 13:21).

Jesus knows that his entire ministry to this point has meaning only in light of his death and resurrection. Jesus' ethical teachings and exemplary lifestyle, of themselves, do not bring salvation; the cross is the reason for the incarnation (Jn 13:27). The hour of God's glorification has come and Jesus prays "Father, glorify your name" (Jn 12:28).

The Father answers immediately; his voice reveals his presence to the bystanders (Jn 12:28–30). Their attention is captured. Jesus now declares, in apocalyptic language, that his hour will be a time of both dethroning and enthroning. The present ruler of this world will be deposed and the Son of Man will be exalted (Jn 12:31–33).

John 12:32 presents the supreme double-meaning of the Gospel: "And I, when I am lifted up from the earth, will draw all people to myself." Ironically, the humiliation of crucifixion is the exaltation of the crucified one. When Jesus is physically hoisted on a cross, he will ascend "from the earth" back to his heavenly origin. From his exalted position, he will attract "all people," whether Jew or Gentile, to come to him in faith.

Jesus' hearers understand "lifting up" only as referring to death. Some protest, saying the Scriptures teach that the Messiah would live forever. Actually, the Old Testament is not explicit in this regard, but they may have had Psalm 89:36 in mind: " . . . His line will continue forever, and his throne endure . . . " In any case, the crucifixion of the Messiah was incompatible with *all* current expectations. Jesus has baffled everyone with his prediction and they ask: "Who is this Son of Man?" (Jn 12:34). What sort of Son of Man would die on a cross?

Jesus does not explain. Instead, he simply invites the audience to follow him. Time is short. The crowd has lived with the light of life for a few years. Jesus has announced his hour and explained its significance; what his hearers do *now* will decide their future. To live as children of light, they *now* must accept the revelation they have been afforded or die engulfed in darkness.

With these final words, Jesus withdraws. People will hear no more from him unless they have chosen to follow him in discipleship.

Unfortunately, few follow. The "Book of Signs" ends with a bleak picture of rejection that John interprets as a fulfillment of prophecy. Not only is unbelief the expected reaction to the saving revelation (Jn 12:38; Isa 53:1), but God intends it:

> He has blinded their eyes
>   and hardened their hearts
> so that they might not look with their eyes,
>   and understand with their heart and turn—
> and I would heal them (Jn 12:40; Isa 6:10).

Both in its original setting in Isaiah and here in John, God intends persistent unbelief to lead to decisive judgment, consequent repentance, and ultimate deliverance. In John's presentation, this unbelief ensures the Son's saving death.

According to John 12:41, the prophet Isaiah anticipated these developments when, in his vision of the divine throne (Isa 6:1–4), he saw Christ. Compare this with John 8:56, where Abraham is said to have seen Jesus' "day." John marshals the support of two of Israel's heroes to affirm the pre-existence and incarnation of the Son of God.

Not all reject Jesus. Some, even among the authorities, believe in him. Still, John criticizes them. Fearing excommunication and loss of reputation, they will not publicly acknowledge their faith. As mentioned in our discussion of John 9:22, the fourth evangelist is particularly sensitive to the reaction of the synagogue against certain Christians and the compromises by other believers who remain "hidden." This is likely due to the experience of the Johannine community itself. In comparison to other Christian groups, the high Johannine view of Christ provoked their early break with Judaism.

Jesus closes the Book of Signs with a summary of his teachings (Jn 12:44–50). Jesus represents God to us; our response to him depicts our response to God. Through his revelation of the Father, the Son offers a dark and dying world light and life. To hear his word and not accept it is to provoke the Father's final judgment.

Conclusion

For three years the Son of God has walked in the world. During that time he has proclaimed, explained, enlightened, corrected, amazed, provoked, healed, and nourished people. He has even resurrected someone from the dead.

He has been praised as a king and condemned as a blasphemer. Some have given their lives to him, while others are planning to take life from him. Now, the forces of unbelief are growing. Darkness, deceit, and death threaten to overwhelm.

Yet, light, truth, and life are still to be found close to Jesus. Before his death, he offers parting words of hope to the faithful. God is still in control and his plan is unfolding as it should.

STUDY QUESTIONS

1. Note three possible allusions to John 13 in the supper at Bethany (Jn 12:1–7).

2. What significance is there to the anointing with nard? What might be a reason Mary anointed his feet instead of his head?

3. Compared to the Synoptic accounts, what is John's stress in his description of the entry into Jerusalem?

4. Why are we told of the visit by Greeks in John 12:20–22?

5. What does Jesus mean when he says people must "hate their life" (Jn 12:25)?

6. As we have seen, the Gospel of John uses words with double-meanings to their full effect. His most important double-meaning occurs in this chapter. What is it? Why is it significant?

7. What *positive* function does John give unbelief?

8. Compare John 12:41 with John 8:56–57. What similarities and differences do you see between the visions of Abraham and Isaiah? How do they relate to John's prologue?

Chapter 11

PARTING WORDS TO THE FAITHFUL: PREPARATIONS FOR DEPARTURE
(John 13)

Introduction

Now before the festival of the Passover, Jesus knew that his hour had come to depart from this world and go to the Father. Having loved his own, he loved them to the end (Jn 13:1).

These two sentences encapsulate the next eight chapters of the Gospel. Although Jesus concludes his public call to light and life, he still has much to say and do among those who have accepted the invitation. Before he returns to his Father, he assures his disciples that the love they share with him will sustain them. Jesus promises that he will always be with his disciples and they will always represent him to the world. Even death will not end their relationship; it will perfect it.

Two scenes in John 13, both set at Jesus' last supper, depict the crucial moments that begin his hour. In the first scene, Jesus washes his disciples' feet. In the second, he makes several startling announcements. These unusual actions and statements convey profound christological, sacramental, soteriological, and ethical truths.

While the Synoptics equate the last supper with the Passover meal, John 13:1 more accurately dates the last supper on the previous day. The issues arising from this discrepancy are too detailed to explore in this context, but it should be noted that both chronologically and theologically John's account is most consistent. Jesus will be put to death on the same day as the paschal lambs. He is the Passover Lamb of God whose blood is shed for the deliverance of God's people.

The Footwashing (Jn 13:2–20)

John is the only evangelist to include the footwashing. Washing one's feet before sitting down to a meal was common practice, but both manner and timing distinguish this particular event.

Normally, guests would use basins of water and towels provided by their host to wash their own feet when they entered the home. No one would wash the feet of another. The rabbis even stipulated that owners could not demean Jewish slaves by requiring them to wash other people's feet (Mekh Exod 21:2.82a).

Jesus shocked everyone by washing the feet of his disciples—all the more since he did so *during* the meal and not upon arrival. Peter's understandable reactions presented the opportunity to explain the spiritual significance of Christ's actions (Jn 13:6–11). They were deliberately orchestrated as a testimony to the nature of Jesus' saving relationship with his disciples. The footwashing was predictive, sacramental, and exemplary.

As Jesus comes closer to the cross, he uses the footwashing to foreshadow his death and resurrection. He is clearly acting in anticipation of the strategic hour (Jn 13:1,3,7). More specifically, the same verbs that describe Jesus taking off and putting on his robe (Jn 13:4,12) also describe the good shepherd laying down and taking up his life (Jn 10:11,15, 17–18). Through the footwashing, Jesus dramatically shows that he will bring cleansing by laying down his life and taking it up again.

Both the context and the content of the footwashing narrative suggest a sacramental understanding. On one hand, the references to water and washing (Jn 13:5–6,8–10) remind some commentators of baptism. The connection, however, is tenuous. On the other hand, it is not surprising to find eucharistic parallels in the footwashing since the other Gospels here recount the institution of the Lord's supper. To participate in the footwashing is to unite with Christ. Just as with the eucharist, words of institution accompany the footwashing. Furthermore, like communion, footwashing joins believers to each other as well as to Christ.

Most striking is Jesus' response to Peter's initial refusal to have his feet washed: "Unless I wash you, you have no share with me" (Jn 13:8). Jesus uses language of bequeathal. The footwashing imparts to the disciple the Son's inheritance from the Father. Because the act prefigures the crucifixion, we may conclude that the only way to share in Jesus' life is to be cleansed by his death and resurrection.

Peter misinterprets Jesus' words and asks for a complete bath! Continuing the metaphor, Jesus explains that spiritual cleansing does not depend on complete comprehension. The disciple's acceptance of Jesus is all that is necessary. What is more, the physical act of washing alone does not spiritually cleanse; Judas, with clean feet, exemplifies one who has rejected a saving relationship.

Jesus inaugurated the observance of the Lord's supper when, after praying and distributing the elements, he commanded: "Do this in remembrance of me" (1 Cor 11:24,25; Lk 22:19–20). Likewise, Jesus makes footwashing an ordinance: " . . . so if I, your Lord and Teacher, have washed your feet, you also ought to wash one another's feet. For I have set you an example, that you should do as I have done to you . . . if you know these things you are blessed if you do them" (Jn 13:14–17).

By setting the example for his disciples, Jesus stresses another relational dimension in the act. Footwashing relates us to each other as well as to Jesus. Just as communion incorporates us into the one body of Christ, so also footwashing unites us in humble mutual service. Our response to others expresses our response to the Father and Son (Jn 13:20).

The account of the footwashing is one of the richest and most overlooked passages of the New Testament. Considering it, we gain insight into the timing and function of Christ's voluntary death. Receiving it, we inherit a share in Christ's life. Practicing it, we express our unity with others who have received him.

As the footwashing narrative comes to a close, Jesus prepares to speak of betrayal among the disciples. He has set the boundaries of true discipleship. His followers may not understand some of the dynamics of Christ's saving work, but they believe God has sent him. In contrast, Judas has not received Christ's cleansing (Jn 13:10–11) and he has scorned the intimacy offered him (Jn 13:18). John assures the reader that Jesus knows Judas will turn on him. He will use the betrayal for his saving work.

Announcements at Supper (Jn 13:21–38)

All four gospels agree that the last supper was the first time Jesus announced the betrayal, although it has been foreshadowed for the reader (Jn 13:2,10–11,18–20). The evangelists also agree that Jesus does not name the traitor. At this point, however, John contributes an independent description of the incident.

John leaves out the institution of the Lord's supper probably because his readers already celebrate the rite and further instruction is unnecessary. He has previously developed the theme somewhat in John 6, as we have seen. In the present narrative he shows that Jesus consciously initiated his hour of glorification.

Though Jesus is in control of his fate, he is still troubled as he predicts his betrayal: "Very truly I tell you, one of you will betray me" (Jn 13:21). The declaration leaves the disciples confused and lost for words.

Now, for the first time, the evangelist mentions the Beloved Disciple. He is lying close to Jesus' chest. The posture, assumed for feasts, is described in a way to suggest intimacy between the Beloved Disciple and Jesus. The same words characterize the Son's relationship with the Father in John 1:18. The bond between Jesus and the true disciple is based on that between God and his Son.

Peter, the next disciple identified in this narrative, typically takes the initiative among his peers. Because of the seating arrangements, he motions to the Beloved Disciple to ask Jesus who the betrayer is. Jesus responds to the private question by dipping a piece of bread in the common dish and offering it to Judas. Apart from the explanation of John 13:26, this common courtesy would not have been conspicuous.

The narrative preserves the tradition that none of the disciples realized the betrayer was Judas (Jn 13:28–29). More than that, it also stresses the active part Jesus played in bringing about his betrayal as part of the hour. Instead of Judas dipping his hand into the bowl, as in Mark 14:20 and Matthew 26:23, in John Jesus dips the morsel himself and hands it to Judas.

Ironically, the gesture of love sets an evil plan in motion. Provoking a crisis of commitment, Jesus says to Judas, "Do quickly what you are going to do" (Jn 13:27). In turn, Judas makes his choice. He takes the bread and leaves immediately.

John ends the scene with a terse sentence: "And it was night" (Jn 13:30). Given the dualism of light and darkness so prevalent in this Gospel, we cannot read this merely as a reference to the time of day. With the permission of Jesus behind him, Judas is embraced by Satan and enters the power of darkness.

Paradoxically, Judas' exit is both tragic and providential. It facilitates the imminent glorification of the Son of Man. Jesus makes his second announcement at supper: he is going away in glory. Because the relationship between the Father and Son is so close, when one is glorified, so is the other (Jn 13:31–32).

Departure means separation from the disciples. Jesus' love for them is evident as he breaks the news: "Little children, I am with you only a little longer. You will look for me; and as I said to the Jews so now I say to you, 'Where I am going you cannot come'" (Jn 13:33). This is the only time the Johannine Jesus uses the endearing term "little children." He knows they will want to follow in devotion, but they will be no more able than those who pursue him for malevolent reasons (Jn 7:32–36). Jesus must go to the cross alone; his death is a departure from the human realm to the divine.

Jesus leaves the disciples with a gift: a "new commandment" to love one another in the same way he has loved them (Jn 13:34). The content of the commandment is not new (cf. Lev 19:18), its relationship to Jesus is. He is the model for the new law and his death empowers its fulfillment.

The new commandment confirms a new covenant between God and his people. Just as the Mosaic law enabled the Israelites to respond to the covenant God established, so this new commandment allows the disciples to respond to their saving relationship with God's Son. By loving one another with Jesus' self-giving love, the disciples proclaim to all people their mutual bond to him.

For Peter, the thought of losing his master obscures any promise the departure offers. Again in his zeal he misunderstands Jesus (cf. Jn 13:6–9). Peter insists that he will accompany him even if it means death. Jesus corrects Peter with words that would come back to haunt the eager follower: "Will you lay down your life for me? Very truly, I tell you, before the cock crows, you will have denied me three times" (Jn 13:38).

At this point it is not the sheep who must die for their shepherd but the shepherd who must lay his life down for the sheep. Before Jesus could become an example to follow he had to go on alone to prepare the way. He predicts that there will be a time for Peter to follow, but it will be "afterward" (Jn 13:36).

As we shall see, Peter does try to follow before his time and instead denies Jesus (Jn 18:15–27). But that is not the end of his story. Peter is finally invited to follow Jesus in a death that would glorify God (Jn 21:18–20). The cross will have made all the difference.

Conclusion

In John 13, Jesus cements his relationship with the disciples while preparing to leave them. At their final meal together, they confront humiliation and glorification, love and betrayal, life and death, and intimacy and distance. The tensions cannot be avoided, they must be endured to be overcome. Eternal glorification, love, life, and intimacy will result.

Although John does not include the institution of the eucharist at the last supper, in its place he recounts how Jesus washed the disciples' feet. In doing so, John draws parallels between communion and footwashing.

Both foreshadow the death of Christ. In particular, the footwashing offers an interpretation of the function of Christ's saving work; he lays down and takes up his life to cleanse those who receive him.

Words of institution are given with both the Lord's supper and footwashing. Observance signifies union with Christ for those who believe. The eucharist and footwashing similarly extend intimacy with Christ to incorporate others in the believing community.

The announcements that follow the footwashing further prepare Jesus' disciples for his hour. Jesus initiates betrayal to lead to the impending glorification of God. His departure will enable deeper relationships for the disciples.

When the disciples hear that Jesus is leaving in the midst of betrayal and denial, their responses vary. Judas makes his choice for evil. Peter remains oblivious to everything but his attachment to the earthly Jesus. His characteristic misunderstandings lead to spiritual lessons for readers with discernment. The Beloved Disciple, now introduced, models a direct, intimate, and insightful relationship with Christ throughout the rest of the Gospel.

STUDY QUESTIONS

1. In what ways does the footwashing of John 13 differ from the typical manner feet were washed in Jesus' time?

2. How does the footwashing foreshadow the death and resurrection?

3. Outline some parallels between the footwashing and the eucharist.

4. List all the predictions Jesus makes in this chapter. Are they all fulfilled in the rest of the Gospel?

5. List all the misunderstandings described in this chapter. Why does John report them? Based on what you read in John 13, is a complete understanding of Christ's teaching a necessary part of true discipleship?

6. In John, how does Jesus identify the betrayer? How is this different from the Synoptic account? What is John emphasizing?

7. Why might it be important to stress that no one else knew about Judas' plan to betray Jesus?

8. Why is the commandment given in John 13:34 "new"?

9. What function does the new commandment have?

Chapter 12

PARTING WORDS TO THE FAITHFUL: PROMISES FOR THE FUTURE
(John 14–16)

Introduction

Jesus knew what his disciples were going through in the aftermath of his shocking announcements. Before the night was over he went on to encourage them, urging them to trust him. He told them that he had to leave; in the end it would be to their advantage (see box).

He was going to the Father to prepare a place for his disciples and he promised to return for them. Then the Father, the Son, and the faithful would live together in unity. In this context Jesus utters his sixth "I am" saying of the gospel: "I am the way, the truth, and the life. No one comes to the Father except through me" (Jn 14:6).

John 15 goes on to offer the final "I am" saying: "I am the true vine, my Father is the vinegrower . . . you are the branches" (Jn 15:1,5). The vineyard metaphor teaches that Jesus connects believers to God, the source of life. They must "remain" in Jesus to survive and flourish. Jesus adds that his followers can only remain in him through the Spirit.

The Holy Spirit is described in a profoundly personal way in this last discourse. Called the "Paraclete," he represents Jesus among the disciples while Jesus is with the Father. The Paraclete reminds them of what Jesus taught. Through them, the Spirit also testifies to the rest of the world, convicting it of the truth of Christ's revelation.

These broad themes are explored in all three chapters of Jesus' final discourse. However, for clarity, we will discuss each one primarily with the chapter in which it is dominant.

THE THEMES OF THE FINAL DISCOURSE
(Jn 14–16)

Access to the Father

"I am the way, the truth, and the life. No one comes to the Father except through me" (Jn 14:6).

Abiding in Jesus

"I am the vine, you are the branches. Those who abide in me and I in them bear much fruit, because apart from me you can do nothing" (Jn 15:5).

Advocacy through the Spirit

"It is to your advantage that I go away, for if I do not go away, the Advocate will not come to you; but if I go, I will send him to you" (Jn 16:7).

Access to the Father (Jn 14)

Jesus tells his disciples that he is going to prepare them a place in his Father's presence. In spite of Jesus' contention that his disciples know the way to the Father's house, Thomas confesses otherwise (Jn 14:4–5). This allows Jesus to be more specific.

The way cannot be drawn on a map; it is embodied in a person. Jesus is the way. He also says that he is the truth and the life (Jn 14:6). In adding these two other elements, he is showing that truth and life characterize the way.

This saying teaches explicitly that Jesus is the exclusive avenue to God the Father. Like the other "I am" sayings, the use of the definite article has the effect of singling out Jesus. He is *the* way. No one can come to the Father except through him.

Two aspects of the concept of truth may come into play in the affirmation that Jesus is the truth. Hebraic thinking about truth involved the idea of reliability or faithfulness. More often in John, though, we find "truth" used in a Greek sense to refer to what is *real* compared to mere appearance (e.g. Jn 4:23–24; 6:55). To say that Jesus is the truth is to say that his revelation affords a completely reliable revelation of reality in its fullest sense.

Jesus is the life. The Father has shared his life with Jesus so that Jesus can give it to others (Jn 5:26; 10:28). We have already seen how this life is eternal and spiritual. From John 14:1–7 we now learn that it is a life lived in God's presence.

When Thomas asked about the way to the Father, Jesus said *he* was the way. Now Philip asks to see the Father (Jn 14:8). Again Jesus presents himself in response:

> Have I been with you all this time, Philip, and you still do not know me? Whoever has seen me has seen the Father. How can you say 'Show us the Father'? Do you not believe that I am in the Father and the Father is in me?

The unity between the Father and Son is the basis for a full revelation of the Father through the Son. To come to the Son is to come to the Father. To see the Son is to see the Father. Jesus does not only show the way, reveal the truth, and offer the life—he alone incarnates these things. He is the only route to full and eternal reality. His unity with the Father makes the Son the actual goal.

Jesus leaves directions for those who trust in him. They are to remain faithful while he goes, follow his teachings, and continue his work in the world as a testimony of their love for him. Because he is going to the Father, he will enable them to carry out this mission to a greater extent than was possible for Jesus during his earthly ministry (Jn 14:12–13).

The disciples will not be left alone in their mission. They will experience the presence of both the Father and the Son through the Spirit. Jesus encourages them one more time with the words "Do not let your hearts be troubled" (Jn 14:27; cf. 14:1) and then concludes his discourse.

The last supper is over. Jesus at last directs his disciples: "Rise, let us be on our way" (Jn 14:31). Because the Gospel now stands with two more discursive chapters, some interpreters read this final sentence figuratively: Jesus is imploring the disciples to begin their spiritual journey. Rather than force this unnatural reading, we should simply regard this final sentence as the end of the original discourse. Before chapters 15–17 were added in the process of composition, the narrative moved directly on to the garden (John 18:1).

Abiding in Jesus (Jn 15)

John 15 opens with Jesus' seventh "I am" saying: "I am the true vine, and my Father is the vinedresser." A few sentences later, in verse 5, he restates the saying with a different emphasis: "I am the vine, you are the branches." Together, the two versions position Jesus as the mediator between the Father and the believer.

Significantly, Jesus claims to be the *true* vine. Imagery in the Old Testament characterizes Israel as a vine or vineyard, and in every instance but Isaiah 27:2–6, Israel the vine is judged unfruitful. The Lord's pronouncement in Jeremiah 2:21 exemplifies the pattern:

> I planted you as a choice vine,
>   from the purest stock.
> How then did you turn degenerate
>   and become a wild vine?

In contrast with the spoiled vine of the nation of Israel, Jesus is the ideal, genuine vine—another example of Jesus superseding Judaism. Now, however, he does not replace simply the temple, the exodus, a feast, a patriarch, or a religious institution. He completely incorporates the new people of God.

From Jesus grow vigorous branches that yield a healthy harvest for God, the vinegrower. John makes a play on words in verses 2 and 3 to extend his metaphor: The Father "removes" (*airei*) unfruitful branches and he "prunes" (*kathairei*) fruitful ones that have already been "cleansed" (*katharoi*).

Both the promise and the warning are unmistakable. An abundant life in the caring hands of the heavenly Father will come, albeit with some personal pruning. Just as surely, those same hands also will take away the dead wood. Apart from Jesus, life withers away. United with Jesus, life flourishes.

Jesus exhorts his disciples to continue to "abide" in him and "bear fruit." In this context, bearing fruit involves keeping Jesus' command and loving one another (Jn 15:12–17; cf. also 13:34). The link between love and obedience has its precedent in the relationship between the Father and Son. The Son expresses his love for the Father by obeying him (Jn 15:10).

The supreme act of love, according to John 15:13, is to die for your friends. When Jesus says this and then immediately calls the disciples his "friends," he is revealing his motive for going to the cross. He is laying down his life because he loves his followers. His self-sacrifice enables and exemplifies the qualities that are to mark Christian relationships: respect, mutuality, intimacy, openness, responsibility, acceptance, and generosity (Jn 15:14–17).

If love is to distinguish interaction among Jesus' disciples, then hate will characterize the world's response to them (Jn 15:18–25). Believers will need everything they can draw from their new relationship with God to withstand the coming wrath. In Jesus' absence, the world's hate will be redirected toward those who represent him.

Fortunately, there is some good news. The disciples will not be abandoned in their crisis. Jesus is going to send a powerful defender to their side (Jn 15:26–27). With the Spirit of truth, they will maintain a faithful witness to the world on Christ's behalf.

Advocacy by the Spirit (Jn 16)

Five passages of the Gospel speak of the Holy Spirit in an exceptional manner (see box). John introduces the "Paraclete." This word, found only in John (cf. also 1 Jn 2:1), has been translated variously: "Counselor," "Comforter," "Helper," or "Advocate." None of the renderings adequately convey the range of meaning implied in John's usage. Consequently, a simple transliteration is recommended.

The Greeks used the word to refer to someone who is called alongside; but the term's distinctive associations arise from the situation in which the person is called. In a courtroom setting, the paraclete was an attorney for the defense. He spoke for the accused. While John reflects some of this intercessory character in his use of the word, he also introduces the role of witness and even prosecutor in his descriptions.

In a religious context, a paraclete might be a "proclaimer" or "exhorter." Specifically, the Johannine Paraclete resembles certain Jewish figures. When the Spirit succeeds Jesus, it mirrors Joshua's succession of Moses, or Elisha taking over from Elijah. The Paraclete's inspiration of the disciples to preach is reminiscent of the Spirit of God coming upon Old Testament prophets.

In later Judaism, Wisdom personified leads the righteous in their struggle against the world, indwelling them, and giving them understanding (e.g. Sir 14:12,26–27,33). The Qumran literature speaks of the "Spirit of truth." He dwells in the hearts of the sectarians, blessing their lives and resisting the spirit of falsehood (1 QS 3:19ff; 4:3–10,17,23–24).

All of these models resemble some aspects of John's Paraclete,

THE PARACLETE IN JOHN

". . . I will ask the Father, and he will give you another Advocate, to be with you forever. This is the Spirit of Truth, whom the world cannot receive, because it neither sees him nor knows him. You know him, because he abides with you, and he will be in you" (Jn 14:16–17).

"I have said these things to you while I am still with you. But the Advocate, the Holy Spirit, whom the Father will send in my name, will teach you everything, and remind you of all that I have said to you" (Jn 14:25–26).

"When the Advocate comes, whom I will send to you from the Father, the Spirit of Truth who comes from the Father, he will testify on my behalf. You also are to testify because you have been with me from the beginning" (Jn 15:26–27).

". . . I tell you the truth: it is to your advantage that I go away, for if I do not go away, the Advocate will not come to you; but if I go, I will send him to you. And when he comes, he will prove the world wrong about sin and righteousness and judgment: about sin, because they do not believe in me; about righteousness, because I am going to the Father and you will see me no longer; about judgment, because the prince of this world has been condemned" (Jn 16:7–11).

"I still have many things to say to you, but you cannot bear them now. When the Spirit of truth comes, he will guide you into all the truth; for he will not speak on his own, but will speak whatever he hears, and he will declare to you the things that are to come. He will glorify me, because he will take what is mine and declare it to you. All that the Father has is mine. For this reason I said that he will take what is mine and declare it to you" (Jn 16:12–15).

though none share his terminology or reflect his overall depth. For this reason, it is best to acknowledge John's presentation of the Paraclete as original.

The mention of "another" Paraclete in John 14:16 implies that Jesus had already fulfilled the role for the disciples. The similarities between Jesus and the Paraclete are impressive. Both are sent by God (Jn 3:17; 15:26). Jesus comes in the Father's name; the Spirit comes in Jesus' name (Jn 5:43; 14:26). Jesus is the truth; the Paraclete is the Spirit of truth (Jn 14:6,17; 15:26; 16:13). Clearly the Paraclete becomes Jesus in the lives of his disciples while Jesus goes to the Father.

With his departure, Jesus asks the Father to send the Spirit to minister to his disciples. The Paraclete will remain with them, teaching and enabling them to testify about Christ to the world. The world will relate to the Paraclete as it does to Jesus and the disciples.

In the last sentence of the Gospel of Matthew, Jesus said to his disciples, " . . . remember, I am with you always, to the end of the age" (Mt 28:20). In John 14:16, he says, "I will ask the Father, and he will give you another Advocate to be with you forever." These are two ways of saying the same thing. The Paraclete is the presence of Jesus in the believer forever (Jn 14:16–17).

The disciples could take heart in the promise of Jesus that he was not actually leaving them; he was going to enter them and reside in them always. Through the Spirit, Jesus remains their constant companion. The rest of the world will neither know him nor see him, but he will be there (Jn 14:17). The disciples can lean on him as opposition arises.

More than a friend who comes alongside during difficult times, the Spirit will be a teacher. Christians are "learners." The word "disciple" (*mathetes*) comes from the verb "to learn" (*manthanein*). The Paraclete continues Jesus' work of making disciples; he teaches them by calling to mind Jesus' words (Jn 14:25–26; 16:12–15). Jesus is the truth (Jn 14:6) and the Spirit leads into all truth (Jn 16:13). Therefore, the Spirit does not teach innovative theology as much as remind Christians of what Jesus has already taught through his word and life. The Paraclete does not teach of his own accord; he reflects Jesus.

Help will be needed especially during persecution. References to apostasy, excommunication, and even martyrdom preface the promise of the Spirit's coming (Jn 16:1–4). These verses are probably to be understood in light of the Johannine community's own experience with the synagogue. In such times, disciples of Christ can rely on the Spirit for the words to say and the courage to speak them (cf. also Jn 9:22).

The Paraclete not only works in the hearts of believers; he also has a message for those who do not accept the claims of Christ: they are wrong. Again John draws on language of the courtroom. The Paraclete cross-examines the world and provides indisputable evidence that leads to a decisive verdict. The Spirit convicts the world of "sin and righteousness and judgment" (Jn 16:8).

To convict the world of sin is to convince people that it is wrong to reject Christ. For John, the ultimate sin is unbelief (Jn 16:9). Such unbelief is reprehensible because it issues from rejection, not ignorance, of the saving revelation. As Jesus has said, "If I had not come and spoken to them, they would not have sin; but now they have no excuse for their sin" (Jn 15:22). The Paraclete exposes those who deliberately have rejected Christ.

Further, the Paraclete convicts the world of righteousness. He works to convince people that even if they are sinful there is someone who is not—Jesus. He alone is righteous and his return to the Father proves it (Jn 16:10). His exaltation on the cross and acceptance by the Father will vindicate him. When he can no longer be seen but only experienced through the Paraclete, the disciples will know he is with the Father.

As the Spirit convicts people of their sinfulness and of Christ's righteousness, they can see the great discrepancy between their status and God's standard. This brings on the conviction of an impending judgment.

Christ's vindication indicts "the ruler of this world" (Jn 16:11). The Paraclete will cause the world to see its precarious situation: it was wrong in its judgment of Christ and now, with Satan, faces condemnation (cf. also Jn 12:31). In other words, the Spirit leads people to see the truth. From there they must make a choice: trusting in Jesus brings salvation, rejecting him brings judgment.

As was true of Jesus' earthly ministry, the Paraclete ultimately works for redemption. Even his work of convicting elicits repentance and faith. It is God's nature to reach out, and through the Paraclete he continues to present the saving work of Christ to the world (Jn 15:26). What is more, the Paraclete does not reach out to the world alone. He works in partnership with believers (Jn 15:27). Together the Spirit and the disciples become an empowered witness for the glorified Christ.

John offers the Bible's most personal depiction of the Spirit. As the Paraclete, he is relational, active, and powerful. Although the Fourth Gospel does not directly address the theological concept of the Trinity, John leads us to identify closely the Holy Spirit with the

Son and the Father. Both the Son and Spirit have been sent by the Father to complete his work in the world and both ultimately glorify him.

Conclusion

Jesus has delivered parting words of both warning and comfort to the disciples. He is going to the Father and leaving them behind to carry on. They must maintain a loving and faithful witness about him to a world that will no longer see him. All the opposition that was previously directed against him will now come their way.

With increased responsibilities come increased resources to meet the challenge. Jesus' presence with the Father means that disciples can ask anything in his name and he will grant it to them (Jn 14:12–14; 15:7; 16:23–24). In the midst of persecution, their joy will be complete (Jn 15:11; 16:20–24). Most importantly, he will come back for them so that they can share in his life with the Father. Meanwhile, they will enjoy yet a deeper relationship with him through the Holy Spirit, whom Jesus will send when he goes to the Father.

STUDY QUESTIONS

1. List all the promises in John 14–16 that are associated with Jesus' departure.

2. List all the warnings in John 14–16 that are associated with Jesus' departure.

3. What does it mean to say that Jesus is the way? How do you relate "way" to "truth" and "life" in John 14:6?

4. In John 14:12–14 Jesus says that his disciples will do greater works than he did because he is going to the Father. How would you interpret this?

5. What do you think Jesus is stressing when he says he is the *true* vine?

6. Based on the teachings of John 15, what does it mean for believers to "bear fruit"? What are the consequences of not bearing fruit?

7. What possible ways are there to translate the word "Paraclete"? Which one do you think is most appropriate?

8. List at least three similarities between Jesus and the Paraclete.

9. What does the Paraclete do in the lives of the disciples?

10. What does it mean to say that the Paraclete "convicts" the world?

Chapter 13

THE HOUR OF GLORIFICATION: ALONE, ON BEHALF OF OTHERS
(John 17)

Introduction

With no more parting words for the disciples, Jesus turns to his heavenly Father. The Son's prayer in John 17 crowns not only the final discourse but his entire teaching. The longest prayer in the New Testament, it highlights the unity between Father and Son as well as the representative nature of Jesus' work.

The prayer of John 17 follows a definite literary convention. The farewell discourses of a dying leader characteristically end in a prayer that expresses the author's paramount hopes for both the leader and his audience. Many parallels exist in both Greek and Hebrew traditions, but the closest is Moses' farewell prayer. In Deuteronomy 32, Moses turns from his people toward heaven and sings a prayer of praise to God. Then, in chapter 33, he prays for the future of the tribes.

Jesus' "last will and testament" revolves around the theme of unity. He cites the unity between the Father and the Son and announces unity between the Son and his disciples before asking for a unity that will span generations of believers. In the course of the prayer, Jesus' prayer offers deep insights into his person and saving work. He spells out the nature of eternal life and defines discipleship.

The prayer defies structural analysis. It weaves together topics so freely that all impositions of a governing order eventually break down. Nevertheless, the prayer can be divided into three parts (see box). Verses 1–5 comprise Jesus' prayer for glorification and focus on the relationship between the Father and Son. A prayer for sanctifica-

THE HOUR OF GLORIFICATION: ALONE, ON BEHALF OF OTHERS (Jn 17)

Jesus has reached out to people, revealed the Father to them, and gathered followers. Now he must leave them all behind and go alone to the cross.

John 17 contains the longest prayer in the New Testament. This "last will and testament" of Jesus highlights the unity between Father and Son as well as the representative nature of Jesus' work. The prayer can be divided into three parts:

Prayer for Glorification (Jn 17:1–5)

This section focuses on the relationship between the Father and Son. Now that the hour of glorification has come, Jesus asks that the Father glorify him so that he can glorify the Father in the world.

Prayer for Sanctification (Jn 17:6–19)

The Son approaches the Father on behalf of the disciples. Jesus knows that when he leaves, his disciples will experience the hatred previously directed toward him. Consequently, he prays for their protection as they carry out their mission in the world.

Prayer for Unity (Jn 17:20–26)

Here Jesus looks to the future, praying for those who will come to believe through the witness of the disciples. He asks that the Father would include believers in the unity that he shares with the Son.

As it began, the prayer ends with references to Jesus' glory and unity with the Father. The circle is completed with all believers drawn into the divine relationship.

tion for his disciples in the world follows in verses 6–19. Verses 20–26 look to the future, praying for those who will come to believe through the word of the disciples. As it began, the prayer ends with references to Jesus' glory and unity with the Father. The circle is completed with all believers drawn into the divine relationship.

Prayer for Glorification (Jn 17:1–5)

Twelve preceding chapters of John have spoken of the glory of God in Jesus. Now the hour of ultimate glorification has come. Jesus asks that the Father glorify him so that he can glorify the Father (Jn 17:1).

In their basic meaning, the words "glory" and "glorify" refer to recognizing with honor and praise. However, as we have already seen concerning John 2:11, the biblical phrase "glory of God" is a technical expression referring to God's eternal mode of existence that becomes visible at strategic moments in the plan of salvation.

John teaches that Christ, before his incarnation, existed in a state of "glory" with the Father "before the world existed" (Jn 17:5). In verse 24 Jesus again alludes to the glory given him "before the foundation of the world" (cf. also Jn 12:41). This existence in "heavenly glory" is the over-arching structure for the Gospel story. The Son left one context of glory, in heaven, to enter a process of "glorification" on earth. This glorification process culminates in Christ's return to his original heavenly glory.

Compare the heavenly glory of the Son with the revelatory glory of the incarnated Jesus: "And the Word became flesh and lived among us, and we have seen his glory, the glory as of the Father's only Son, full of grace and truth" (Jn 1:14; cf. also 2:11 and 7:39). God's glory has descended to earth for all to see. In his glorification, Jesus is the manifestation of the otherwise invisible God.

Jesus' vocabulary marks crucifixion as a high point in the revelation of glory. His death means glorification (Jn 13:31; 17:1). He calls the crucifixion his "exaltation" (Jn 3:14; 8:28; 12:32–36). The double meaning of exaltation not only points to the integral role the cross plays in Christ's saving work, but also identifies Jesus as the object of worship. On the cross, Jesus displays God's saving presence before all people.

Because such passages as John 17:5 appear to teach that the human Son of God did not exist in the same state of glory as the heavenly Son, some theologians postulate a heavenly glory distinct in essence from the earthly glory. This differentiation is not necessary. "Glory" is used throughout the Bible, both of God's state of being, and of episodic manifestations of that same state. So, too, with Christ, there is continuity between his heavenly glory and its earthly expressions; only time, space, and human comprehension limit the revelation of glory to the people.

In the middle of his request for glorification, Jesus declares his most concise definition of eternal life: " . . . And this is eternal life, that they may know you, the only true God, and Jesus Christ whom you have sent" (Jn 17:3). Far from being an unrelated gloss, as some scholars assert, the statement is integral to this section. The perception of the glory of God in Jesus leads to eternal life for believers.

Jesus has been sent to reveal God, that we might know him. Understanding the revelation means more than knowing *about* God. True to the biblical sense of "knowing" someone, to know God is to have an intimate personal relationship with both the Father and the Son. Such a relationship with God is eternal life.

In his glorification, Jesus represents God to the disciples. This is clear in the "giving" that Jesus describes in his prayer. The Father gives life to the Son, the Son shares it with his disciples (Jn 17:2). The Father gives his words to the Son, the Son passes them on (Jn 17:7-8). The Father gives glory to the Son, the Son gives it to believers (Jn 17:22).

The direction of giving reverses in the next section of the prayer. Jesus now presents the disciples to God, giving them over to the Father's service.

Prayer for Sanctification (Jn 17:6-19)

In John 17:6-8, Jesus explains why he is praying for the disciples. They belong to God and they now know him. Jesus has spoken the word of God and the disciples have accepted it as such. They recognize that the Father has sent him. The disciples now participate in the eternal life of God; in the Son's absence they will need the Father's help.

The Son tells the Father, "I have made your name known . . . the words that you gave me I have given to them" (Jn 17:6,8). Considering the distinctive use of the "I am" formula in this gospel, Jesus may be referring to "Yahweh" when he speaks of a name in John 17:6. More generally, though, in semitic thought a person's name disclosed his or her character. Jesus made God's name known by revealing

God's nature. Clearly the words of Jesus do not simply convey information; they communicate personality and bring salvation.

The disciples "know in truth" and "believe" that Jesus was sent by God (Jn 17:8). The verbs are parallel and should be understood synonymously (cf. Jn 6:69; 10:38; 16:30), describing more than the acceptance of propositions. The will, as well as the intellect, is engaged.

We have already noted that true knowledge of someone requires an intimate relationship. Similarly, to believe is to entrust oneself obediently to the one in whom faith is placed. The disciples have trusted Jesus to bring them into a relationship with God and they have "kept" his word (Jn 17:6).

In contrast, the world has not embraced Jesus. It hates him and his disciples. While Jesus was in the world, he was able to guard them. Now that he is leaving, the disciples alone will reflect his glory and the world will turn on them. They will become the focal point for its hatred. More than ever, they will need God's protection lest they be lost.

One disciple, Judas, has already been lost (Jn 17:12). Here he is literally called "the son of destruction." Some interpreters equate this phrase with its use as a title for the eschatological antichrist in 2 Thessalonians 2:3. They then see this as evidence of John's realized eschatology: Judas was the antichrist that marked the end of the age. However, a single reference in 2 Thessalonians cannot be conclusive. It is better to read John's phrase as a simple affirmation that Judas was destined to perish as part of the saving plan. This is not the first time John has tried to show that the choice of Judas was not an ignorant mistake (Jn 6:70–71; 12:4–8; 13:21–30).

Jesus makes clear distinctions in his prayer: he stipulates that he is not praying for the world, but for the disciples (Jn 17:9). The faithful need to be guarded from the world (Jn 17:11–12). They do not belong in the world (Jn 17:14,16).

Still, the Johannine Jesus is not an extreme sectarian. Many other statements in the gospel show that the "world" is also the object of God's love and the recipient of the offer of salvation (cf. Jn 1:29; 3:16–17; 4:42; 6:33,51; 8:12; 12:47). Here, though, the term "world" refers to humanity reacting against God's overtures.

Also explicit in this prayer is the disciples' mission in the world; they must remain for that reason. Jesus prays "I am not asking you to take them out of the world, but I ask you to protect them . . . As you have sent me into the world, so I have sent them into the world" (Jn 17:15,18). Rather than choosing to live in isolation from the world, they are to be protected so that they can work in it. Ultimately, Jesus prays that the world may believe through the disciples (Jn 17:21,23).

In John 17:19, Jesus asks the Father to "sanctify" the disciples: "Sanctify them in the truth; your word is truth. As you have sent me into the world, so I have sent them into the world. And for their sakes I sanctify myself, so that they also may be sanctified in truth." Literally, Jesus is asking that the disciples be "made holy" in the truth of God's word. Jesus also says he sanctifies *himself*, so this request is neither to save the disciples nor make them morally pure. To be sanctified in the truth is to be "set apart" or dedicated as witnesses to the saving revelation. In their consecration they join not only Jesus but also the "holy" Father (Jn 17:11).

Prayer for Unity (Jn 17:20–26)

Jesus assumes success in the shared mission. He looks at those who will come to believe through the witness of the disciples he is leaving behind (Jn 17:20). He prays for their unity.

The concern for unity that dominates this section of the prayer echoes Jesus' sentiments of John 10:16: "I have other sheep that do not belong to this fold. I must bring them also, and they will listen to my voice. So there will be one flock, one shepherd." Jesus is now praying for these "other sheep" and, by doing so, includes every subsequent believer.

Johannine Christians must have found the prayer particularly poignant. During their first generation, they remained aloof, separated from other Christians. Later, internal divisions plagued the community (1 Jn 2:19) and finally a remnant merged with the mainstream of the church. The prayer of John 17 saw the community through its struggles.

Goodwill and human effort cannot establish the unity of which Jesus speaks; he asks the Father for it. This unity is not a fleeting harmony, dependent on the will of its participants. This unity is an objective reality that has its source in God. Because the Father and Son are one, the disciples can be one with each other and with God (Jn 17:21–23).

Taking the relationship between the Father and Son as the model, Christian unity is to be one of mutual love, purpose, word, and action. It is anachronistic to argue that this prayer calls for institutional or denominational unity, but it does describe a phenomenon that is complete and obvious to the world.

The world needs to witness our unity so that it will believe that God sent Jesus (Jn 17:21). Because we live in unity with the Father and Son, we can reflect their glory in the world (Jn 17:22). Our love for one another will show the world that we are loved by God just as Jesus was loved (Jn 17:23). The love we share with God appeals to the world and verifies Christ's work.

The prayer culminates with John 17:24. Jesus' vision encompasses the past, present, and future when he prays, "Father, I desire that those also, whom you have given me, may be with me where I am, to see my glory, which you have given me because you loved me before the foundation of the world." In language that reiterates major themes, Jesus offers a future hope to all disciples. They will be brought into the presence of the pre-existent, eternal and glorified Son of God. John's eschatology is yet to be fully realized.

Verses 25–26 emphasize the justice inherent in Jesus' request. Addressing the Father as "righteous" or "just," Jesus implies that he is not asking for any unfair bias in favor of the disciples. Jesus has revealed God to everyone. The world has acknowledged neither the Father nor the Son, but the disciples have. Jesus prays for them because they have accepted the revelation.

Conclusion

This prayer is an inspiring example of Jesus' self-understanding and love for others. With death looming, his foremost concern is for believers. In the personal crisis of the moment, he looks to the future. One cannot read the intercession without sensing the needs of the Johannine community. Wrestling with internal divisions and facing external threats, they will cling to their Lord's words in John 17. What is more, these words are just as relevant today, for we, too, are included in his prayer and share the same needs.

Jesus prays for unity. The basis of this unity is the glory that the Father and Son have shared eternally. Those who recognize this glory are drawn in and set apart to reflect to the world for succeeding generations.

Preparations are complete. Jesus is ready to present himself for glorification on the cross.

STUDY QUESTIONS

1. The Son of God exists in glory in two different spheres. How would you relate his heavenly glory with his earthly glory?

2. What function does the process of Jesus' glorification on earth have? How can the glory of God be seen today?

3. According to John, what does it mean to "know" someone? What does it mean to "believe" in someone? How do these concepts compare with modern Western notions of knowledge and belief?

4. Why does Jesus pray for the disciples but not for the world? Is he being fair? Is he unconcerned for the world?

5. Why do the disciples need the Father's protection?

6. What does it mean, in Jesus' prayer, to be "sanctified" by God's word of truth?

7. What is the basis for unity in the church? What function does Christian unity have in the world?

8. Isolate two passages in John 17 that might indicate John's eschatological perspective. Based on your interpretation of these, would you consider John's eschatological hope to be fully realized?

Chapter 14

THE HOUR OF GLORIFICATION: CRUCIFIXION AND EXALTATION
(John 18–19)

Introduction

Without chapters 18–20, the Gospel of John would not be a Gospel. From his first chapter, John had the cross in mind. All fears are faced; all hopes are realized. We have reached the climax of the narrative. God in the flesh leaves earth and returns to glory in heaven, opening the way for believers to follow.

The literary devices that foreshadowed this hour now describe it. As so often before, here when Jesus is put on trial he cross-examines his accusers. Just as at Jacob's well (Jn 4), teaching in the temple (Jn 7), and healing the blind man (Jn 9), scenes on two stages dramatize Christ's encounter with the world. John continues to use irony, double meaning, misunderstandings, and symbolism.

Those who assume power do not really have it; Jesus has control. He is crowned the King of the Jews. He is not simply lifted up on a cross; he is exalted before the world. His blood is shed as the new Passover Lamb. In the midst of threatening darkness, a glimmer of faith shines. That ember will glow until the resurrection fans it to flame.

The Arrest (Jn 18:1–11)

After his prayer, Jesus and the disciples crossed the Kidron valley and entered a garden just to the east of Jerusalem. The place was a favorite gathering spot for the group, making it easy for Judas to lead the arresters directly to Jesus.

Of the four evangelists, only John tells us that Roman soldiers accompanied the Jewish temple police. This is the first of several places where John highlights Roman political involvement. Jew and Gentile unite against Jesus for both religious and political reasons. Technically, a "detachment" of soldiers numbered 600, but John should not be interpreted literally at this point. It is better to assume that a smaller group of soldiers accompanied the religious authorities to prevent violence.

There are no surprises for Jesus. He takes the initiative and presents himself, again employing the "I am" formula (Jn 18:5). On the surface, he is simply identifying himself as Jesus of Nazareth. However, when he makes the pronouncement, the forces step back and fall to the ground (Jn 18:6)! The point is unmistakable: whether or not they understand, the arresting officers are in the presence of God. For emphasis, John includes the "I am" phrase three times in the narrative (Jn 18:5,6,8).

Because Jesus does not resist arrest, he can ask that his disciples be spared. John presents this as a fulfillment of prophecy (Jn 18:9). Notably, the prophecy is not from the Old Testament, but is by Jesus, found in John 17:12. Later in this chapter John will record the realization of another one of Jesus' predictions (cf. Jn 18:32 to 12:32–33). The fulfillment language in these references shows that John ranked Jesus' words with Old Testament Scripture.

The police move in. With well-meant heroism, Peter brandishes a sword to defend his Master, cutting off the ear of Malchus, a slave of the high priest's. Instead of thanking Peter, Jesus says, "Put your sword back into its sheath. Am I not to drink the cup that the Father has given me?" (Jn 18:11). Peter does not yet comprehend God's saving plan.

Interestingly, there are several descriptive details in the account of the arrest that indicate eyewitness material independent of the Synoptics. Only John mentions the *Kidron valley*, Roman soldiers, and lamps and torches. While all four Gospels tell us about the servant's ear, only John names Peter and Malchus.

Interpreters debate the significance of these details, but the main theme of John's arrest account is clear. Jesus knowingly and voluntarily turns himself over to his opponents. He is not surrendering to the forces of darkness; he is surrendering to the plan of God.

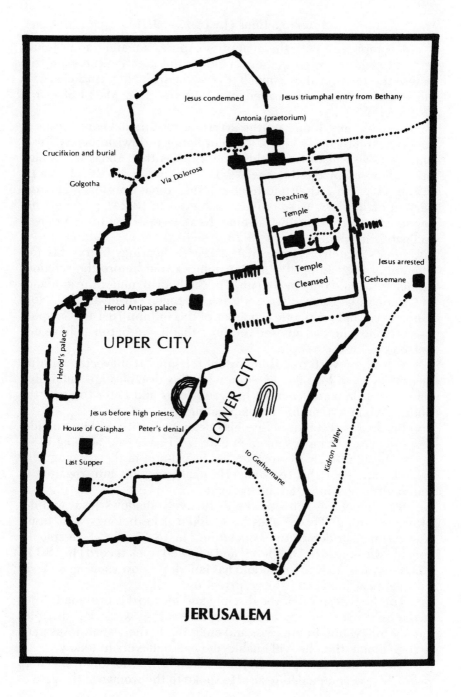

JERUSALEM

Interrogations (Jn 18:12–19:16)

A comparison with the Synoptics exposes a major gap in John's account of Jesus' interrogations: he does not mention the main trial before the Jewish ruling council, the Sanhedrin. No formal charge is laid and no witnesses are called (cf. Mt 26:57–27:2; Mk 14:53–15:1; Lk 22:54–23:1).

Instead, only John says the arresting officers delivered Jesus to Annas, who obviously held a place of honor in Jewish society. Josephus, a Jewish historian of the time, reports that Annas was a high priest deposed by the Romans in A.D. 15 (Ant. 18:2.1.26; cf. also Lk 3:2 and Acts 4:6). After questioning Jesus, Annas transfers him to the current high priest, his son-in-law Caiaphas (Jn 18:24). John does not report an interrogation by Caiaphas. Next we read that Jesus is moved to Pilate's headquarters (Jn 18:28) (see box).

John's sketchy version of the Jewish hearings betray his low opinion of their integrity. At this point, a trial before the religious authorities could only be a sham. The Sanhedrin, under the guidance of Caiaphas, had already passed their sentence (Jn 11:45–53). Note the satirical and prophetic reminder of this in John 18:14: "Caiaphas was the one who had advised the Jews that it was better to have one person die for the people."

Still, the Jewish trial is important for John. It shows the faithfulness of Jesus to his mission, even when his disciples are unfaithful. John sets a dramatic contrast between Jesus and Peter to make the point. Two investigations are happening.

Inside, Jesus stands before his questioners with nothing to hide. Jesus declares "I have spoken openly . . . I have said nothing in secret" (Jn 18:20). Everyone who has heard him in the synagogue or temple can report his teaching. He challenges his interrogators to find fault in anything that he has said.

Simultaneously, outside, Peter furtively shadows Jesus and denies everything. Three times he is asked if he belongs with Jesus. Three times he denies the association (Jn 18:17,25,27). In spite of specific warnings (Jn 13:36–38) and a flawed track record (Jn 18:11–12), Peter has tried to follow and has failed. He now vanishes and will not reappear until after the resurrection.

The juxtaposition of the disciple and his Lord is profound. Jesus is the only one who can complete God's saving work. His disciples cannot follow him to the cross and on to the Father—yet. Jesus must first go alone; then he will enable and call believers to follow.

The "other disciple" of John 18:15–16, who knew the high priest, also accompanied Jesus. He spoke to the woman at the gate to allow Peter into the courtyard. The passage says nothing else about this disciple. Traditionally, readers have identified him as the Beloved Disciple and a careful comparison with other passages, especially John 20:3–10, support this conclusion.

If the Beloved Disciple is present in John 18, then this is the second of five scenes in which he joins Peter (Jn 13:23–25; 18:15–17; 20:3–10; 21:7; 20–26). His actions are always peripheral to the plot, but he often displays faithful insight. The readers cannot fail to identify with him as they interact with the narrative.

Most of the trial narrative concerns Pilate's interaction with Jesus and the Jews (Jn 18:28–19:16). Again the narrative creates dramatic contrast by shifting from inside to outside. Seven scenes alternate to take the reader from Pilate's introduction to the case to his sanctioning of the crucifixion (see box). Pontius Pilate shrinks in stature from the impartial Roman governor of Judea to an intimidated subject of mob rule. All the while, he stands in the shadow of the true King of the Jews.

Kingship is the issue in the trial. The Jews accused Jesus of claiming to be King of the Jews, a treasonous crime punishable by crucifixion under Roman law. More than stoning, crucifixion would signify for the Jews that God had cursed Jesus (Deut 21:23). John, by contrast, sees the Jewish insistence on crucifixion as another fulfillment of Jesus' words (Jn 18:33).

Pilate asks his prisoner if he is the King of the Jews. In response, Jesus admits he is a king but his kingdom is not of this world. Pilate does not perceive the truth of Jesus' claims, but neither does he perceive Jesus to be a threat. He derisively proclaims him "King of the Jews" (Jn 18:39; 19:14,19,22) yet declares three times "I find no case against him" (Jn 18:38; 19:4,6).

With corresponding blind ridicule, the soldiers use thorns to crown Jesus "King of the Jews" and then hit him. Presenting the pathetic figure before the Jews, Pilate heaps the scorn higher: "Here is the man!" (Jn 19:5). Pilate sees nothing more than a humiliated, harmless mortal. The Jews insist he must be put to death "because he claimed to be the Son of God" (Jn 19:7).

The mention of the Son of God stops Pilate short: he "was more afraid than ever" (Jn 19:8). Is he afraid that he has been caught in the trap of cloaking religious retribution in political uniform? The way John describes it, it is more likely that Jesus' transcendent demeanor through the ordeal has already piqued Pilate's suspicions of Jesus' divine origin. Pilate asks Jesus, "Where are you from?" (Jn 19:9). He has asked the most pertinent question one could ask the Johannine Son of God.

THE SEVEN SCENES OF THE TRIAL BEFORE PILATE

". . . Then they took Jesus from Caiaphas to Pilate's headquarters . . ." (Jn 18:28)

INSIDE	OUTSIDE
	Scene 1: Pilate went out and asked "What accusation do you bring against this man?" (Jn 18:29–32).
Scene 2: Pilate enters and asks Jesus, "Are you the King of the Jews?" Jesus acknowledges his kingship (Jn 18:33–38).	
	Scene 3: Pilate tells the Jews "I find no case against him." He offers to release Jesus according to the Passover custom. The crowd refuses (Jn 18:38–40).
Scene 4: Pilate has Jesus flogged. The soldiers mock him saying. "Hail, King of the Jews!" (Jn 19:1–3).	
	Scene 5: Pilate repeats "I find no case against him." He brings Jesus out and says "Here is the man." The crowd demands, "Crucify him!" (Jn 19:4–7).
Scene 6: Pilate becomes afraid at the report of his claim to be the Son of God. He asks Jesus, "Where are you from?" He tries to release Jesus but instead bows to political pressure (Jn 19:8–12).	
	Scene 7: Pilate brings Jesus out and pronounces his judgment: "Here is your King!" The chief priests say, "We have no king but the emperor." Pilate hands Jesus over to be crucified (Jn 19:13–16).

Pilate had not earlier heard the truth (Jn 18:37–38) and so Jesus does not answer now. Pilate's threats do not shake Jesus. The Son of God replies: "You would have no power over me unless it was given you from above . . . " (Jn 19:11). After this response, Pilate decides to release Jesus.

By now, though, Pilate has been trapped by his own maneuvering. He cannot release Jesus and still maintain control over his province. As with all who meet Jesus, Pilate must ultimately decide for or against Jesus. He makes his choice and brings Jesus out to the mob.

Out above the crowd, Pilate takes his place on the judge's bench (Jn 19:13). "Shall I crucify your King?" he asks. Provoked, the Jews blaspheme: "We have no king but the emperor" (Jn 19:15). Like Pilate, they have been caught in their manipulations. By rejecting Jesus, the Jews have traded all messianic hope in exchange for a Gentile oppressor. They have rushed into the arms of another king rather than accept God's anointed one.

The verdict comes down; Pilate hands Jesus over to the Jews for crucifixion (Jn 19:16).

The Crucifixion (Jn 19:16–27)

The climax of John's Gospel is succinct. Rather than detracting from the importance of the crucifixion, the brevity of its narration accents its accomplishment. John's perspective emerges clearly in a comparison with the Synoptic accounts. He selectively downplays the suffering and sadness of Jesus' death, real as it is, and stresses his exaltation as King.

Jesus carries his cross to "The Place of the Skull" (Jn 19:17), so called because of the skull-like shape of the site. There the cross-bar Jesus carried would be joined to one of the stakes set in the hill. No mention is made of how, along the way, the soldiers conscript Simon the Cyrene to carry Jesus' cross (Mk 15:21). John stresses what Jesus *does* more than what is *done to him* throughout this narrative.

A single sentence reports the actual crucifixion (Jn 19:18). The exaltation of the King is proclaimed by the sign affixed to Jesus' cross: "The King of the Jews." Written in Aramaic, Latin, and Greek, the sign places the whole world under its claim. Pilate has had the last word to the chagrin of the Jews. What is meant as a mockery stands true.

As was customary, the four soldiers who conducted the execution divided the victim's possessions among themselves. As mundane as this practice might have seemed to onlookers, in it John sees the fulfillment of Scripture. He focuses attention on the seamless tunic that was worn next to the skin under one's robe. Not wanting to tear the tunic, the soldiers decide to gamble to see which one will get it. Psalm 22:18, which John quotes, is fulfilled.

Many interpreters have further suggested that John understood the seamlessness symbolically. Since the high priest's outer robe was seamless, perhaps John is highlighting the priestly function of Jesus. Or, the seamless tunic may represent the unity of the church. More recently some have suggested that God's protection is symbolized: while Jesus, in his humanity, is stripped bare, his closest piece of clothing remains intact. Any one of these symbolic readings is possible, though none are convincing.

Four women gather at the foot of the cross, standing in contrast to the four soldiers. One of them, Jesus' mother, was standing beside the Beloved Disciple. When Jesus saw them, he made two poignant pronouncements (Jn 19:26–27). By making the Beloved Disciple Mary's son, and she his mother, Jesus not only made provision for his mother's care; he also proclaimed that the crucifixion marks not the end, but the beginning of new relationships in the family of God.

The Death and Burial (Jn 19:28–42)

Even in his death, Jesus controls his destiny. A sense of accomplishment pervades his final moments alive (Jn 19:28–30). Only John tells us he announces his thirst and consciously receives the wine vinegar to fulfill Scripture. Jesus *knew* that his work was finished (Jn 19:28) and he says so (Jn 19:30). In an act of completion, he bows his head and gives up his spirit.

The offering of wine vinegar, the drink of common people, fulfills Psalm 69:21: " . . . for my thirst they gave me vinegar to drink." Curiously, the sponge full of sour wine is hoisted "on a branch of hyssop" (Jn 19:29). The Synoptics speak of a "stick" (Mt 27:48; Mk 15:36).

Hyssop was a small leafy plant that would not serve well as a hoist for a wet sponge. The plant, however, did have one distinctive function: a hyssop bunch was dipped in the blood of the slain Passover Lamb for sprinkling on the doorframe (Ex 12:22). Here is the key to its interpretation in John 19:29. Jesus is the Passover Lamb who sheds his blood for the deliverance of God's people.

This is just one of several Passover references made during Jesus' "hour." The Jews did not enter Pilate's headquarters for Jesus' interrogation "so as to avoid ritual defilement and to be able to eat the

Passover" (Jn 18:28). Pilate gave them the option of freeing Jesus as part of a Passover custom (Jn 18:38).

More to the point, the very hour that priests began slaughtering Passover lambs, noon on the day of Preparation, Jesus was handed over to be crucified (Jn 19:14). Finally, contrary to normal crucifixion practice *and* a special request from the Jews, Jesus' legs were not broken (Jn 19:31–36). Exodus 12:46 and Numbers 9:12, now fulfilled in Jesus (Jn 19:31), stipulate that the bones of the Passover lamb cannot be broken (cf. also Ps 34:20).

Instead of breaking Jesus' legs, a soldier speared Jesus' side. This, too, is a fulfillment of Scripture (Jn 19:37; cf. Zech 12:10). However, the significance of the action runs even deeper. An eyewitness, probably the Beloved Disciple, solemnly testifies that he saw blood and water flow from Jesus' pierced side (Jn 19:34–35; cf. 21:24). Clearly, the evangelist considers this a crucial observation—but why?

An apologetic concern is foundational: John is saying that Jesus certainly suffered physical death. This reality would later be challenged because of the empty tomb. On a secondary level, a small minority of scholars see the "blood and water" as allusions to the eucharist and baptism. In this view, Jesus' death empowers the sacraments.

If John intends a secondary meaning, however, it more likely relates to the giving of the Spirit. John 7:38 says that living waters will flow from Jesus' heart. John tells us that these living waters represent the Spirit that will be given when Jesus is glorified (Jn 7:39). His death on the cross, confirmed by the shedding of blood, glorifies him. Now the Spirit flows from his heart.

Normally, after a crucifixion the corpse would be left for the vultures but the Jews did not want a body on the cross for the coming festal sabbath (Jn 19:31). Two secret believers secure permission from Pilate to bury Jesus. Notably, both Nicodemus (Jn 3:1–10; 7:50–52) and Joseph of Arimathea are members of the Sanhedrin (Mt 27:57; Mk 15:43; Lk 23:50).

The wealthy benefactors spare no expense: they use more than a hundred pounds of spices and place his body in a new garden tomb. The extravagance is reminiscent of Mary's anointing of Jesus (Jn 12:3–8). Jesus, the King of the Jews, has been honored with a fitting burial.

Conclusion

In his arrest, interrogations, and crucifixion, Jesus is no hapless victim; he is the reigning King. The cross is his throne. Nothing happened as a contingency; God orchestrated everything as he worked out his plan for salvation. Allusions to the Passover, the fulfillment of Scripture, and the completion of Christ's work abound.

Several times in earlier chapters John has stated that Jesus must be "lifted up" to draw all people to him (Jn 3:14; 8:28; 12:32,34). The phrase signifies both exaltation and crucifixion. By understanding this double meaning, we can see the cross as the moment of Jesus' glorification. Further, as chapter 20 will confirm, the exaltation on the cross also marks the point of departure and ascension to the Father.

STUDY QUESTIONS

1. The theme of fulfillment runs throughout John 18–19. List the Old Testament passages that John sees fulfilled in the arrest, crucifixion, and death in Jesus.

2. In two other places, John says that Jesus' own words were fulfilled. List them and comment on the significance of this fulfillment language.

3. Who was Caiaphas? Why does John mention his earlier role in the Gospel?

4. What theological significance do you see in John's account of Peter's denials?

5. Note three scenes in John 18–19 in which the Beloved Disciple may have appeared. What function might he have in these scenes?

6. Although it is never stated explicitly, what is the charge against Jesus the Jews bring before Pilate? Show how John, using irony, develops the charge into a motif.

7. What theological significance is there to the three languages of the sign on the cross?

8. List three possible symbolic interpretations of the incident concerning Jesus' seamless tunic.

9. List all the allusions to the Passover in John 18–19.

Chapter 15

THE RESURRECTION APPEARANCES: "THAT YOU MAY BELIEVE" (John 20)

Introduction

History and faith come together in John's account of the resurrection appearances. As do the Synoptics, John verifies the evidences of the empty tomb and the abandoned grave clothes with the witness of Mary Magdalene and Peter. Then John proceeds with a series of distinctive vignettes in which Jesus encounters individuals, meeting them at their level of insight and need, so that each may respond in faith (see box).

The Beloved Disciple "meets" Jesus in the empty tomb; Mary meets Jesus in her mourning; other disciples meet Jesus in their fear; and Thomas meets him in his doubt. John clarifies the theme of this chapter with Jesus' response to Thomas: "Have you believed because you have seen? Blessed are those who have not seen yet have come to believe" (Jn 20:29). John 20 is a call for the reader to respond, as did the Beloved Disciple, in faith without seeing.

A striking feature of this chapter is the profound change in Jesus. He now exists in a glorified state that transcends earthly limitations: Mary must not hold on to him; he mysteriously enters locked rooms; and he can now give the promised Spirit and thereby indwell his disciples.

The Grounds of Faith (Jn 20:1–8)

All four Gospels name Mary Magdalene as the first to find the tomb empty, although other women were present (Mt 28:1; Mk 16:1; Lk 24:10). In Matthew, Luke, and John, the women report their dis-

THE RESURRECTION APPEARANCES IN JOHN

Mary Magdalene reports the empty tomb to Peter and the Beloved Disciple, they investigate (Jn 20:1–10). The Beloved Disciple comes to resurrection faith based on the evidence of the empty tomb. Following this, the resurrected Lord appears four times:

Mary Magdalene in Her Mourning (Jn 20:11–18)

Outside the empty tomb, Jesus meets Mary. She mistakes him for the gardener until he calls her by name. Jesus sends her with the good news of the resurrection to the disciples.

The Disciples in Their Fear (Jn 20:19–23)

The disciples are meeting together behind closed doors when Jesus appears in their midst. He says, "Peace be with you," commissions them, and gives them the Holy Spirit.

Thomas in His Doubt (Jn 20:24–29)

Again in a locked room, Jesus comes to the disciples. This time, Thomas is present. He again greets them with "Peace be with you" and shows Thomas his crucifixion wounds. Thomas confesses "My Lord and my God."

Jesus pronounces a beatitude: "Blessed are those who have not seen and yet have come to believe" (Jn 20:29).

The Disciples in Galilee (Jn 21:1–23)

Peter and six other disciples, including the Beloved Disciple, have gone fishing. Jesus appears on the shore and enables a miraculous catch of fish. The Beloved Disciple realizes who is on the shore and when he tells Peter, Peter jumps overboard and swims to meet Jesus.

Jesus restores Peter after his denials and gives him a pastoral commission. The deaths of both Peter and the Beloved Disciple are discussed.

covery to the disciples. Only Luke and John describe a subsequent visit to the tomb by any disciples other than the women (Lk 24:12,24; Jn 20:3–10). Faith in the resurrection was not part of the traditions of the empty tomb as they originally circulated. The women left afraid the body was stolen; Peter departed from the tomb wondering what had happened. The Gospel of John, however, develops the empty tomb into an occasion for faith.

Sunday morning, while it was still dark, Mary Magdalene came to the tomb to discover that it was open. Because the Synoptics tell us that Mary came at sunrise (Mt 28:1; Mk 16:2; Lk 24:1), we should read the mention of darkness as another of John's many symbolic comments. Mary was in mourning; as yet, none of the disciples believed that Christ was resurrected. All were still walking in spiritual darkness.

Upon discovering the open tomb, Mary ran to report the news to Peter and the Beloved Disciple: "They have taken the Lord out of the tomb, and we do not know where they have laid him" (Jn 20:2; cf. 20:13). Her words suggest that others were with her. More important, however, they imply that she thought the body of Jesus was stolen. She may not have been accusing specific enemies of Jesus bent on discrediting him and his disciples; tomb robbery was a frequent crime in the region. Roman law was soon to impose capital punishment to curb it.

Peter and the Beloved Disciple start running to the tomb together, but both verse 4 and 8 say that the Beloved Disciple reaches the site first. Oddly, he stops short, outside the tomb. Peter arrives and enters the tomb immediately. This description is not simply evidence of the Beloved Disciple's youthful vigor and Peter's characteristic impetuosity, as a few scholars maintain. John is carefully ordering the arrivals and entrances to build suspense as he leads to a climax.

Before the Beloved Disciple enters the tomb, John details Peter's discovery (Jn 20:6–7): "He saw the linen wrappings lying there, and the cloth that had been on Jesus head, not lying with the linen wrappings but rolled up in a place by itself."

A few scholars suggest that the clothes remained in a bodily form, like an empty shell lying in position where Jesus had lain before his resurrection. If this were so, Peter would likely have concluded that Jesus was resurrected. Instead, Peter walked home puzzled (Lk 24:12). A more considered interpretation is that the clothes were folded in a tidy arrangement. In either case, clearly the body of Jesus was not stolen. What hurried robber would undress the body and neatly fold the clothes?

Mary Magdalene and Peter together fulfill an important function at the grave site. Unaffected by anticipation or incipient faith, their witness is an objective report; the facts they recount lead to faith. In turn, Peter's partner, the Beloved Disciple, models resurrection faith that is grounded in the foundational evidence.

The Responses of Faith (Jn 20:8–29)

The remainder of John 20 relates, in four scenes, how certain disciples came to faith in the resurrected Jesus. The hero of the Johannine community is the first to do so.

The Beloved Disciple (Jn 20:8–10)

The Beloved Disciple came to the proper conclusion based on empirical evidence of the empty tomb: he believed (Jn 20:8). What is more, he had not seen his resurrected Lord, nor did he have the confirmation that Christian reflection on the Old Testament would later afford (Jn 20:9).

It does not say *what* the Beloved Disciple believed and verse 9 suggests that his faith was not yet fully formed. However, we cannot accept the interpretation first proposed by Augustine that the Beloved Disciple merely believed Mary's report that the body was gone. Such a conclusion trivializes John's concept of belief and the example he makes of the Beloved Disciple. John has constructed his narrative to bring his readers to the same point of faith. They, too, have not seen the risen Christ, but are still asked to emulate the Beloved Disciple's response to the evidence of the resurrection.

John intends no contrast between the Beloved Disciple's faith and Peter's apparent lack of it. Rather, the two disciples play complementary roles in a unified summons to resurrection faith. One is a witness, the other a believer. Peter, *not* the Beloved Disciple, verifies the conditions of the empty tomb. The Beloved Disciple, *not* Peter, trusts those conditions to be a sign from God. The scene ends as the disciples walk off to their homes (Jn 20:10). The first call to faith is complete.

Mary Magdalene (Jn 20:11–18)

Next, Mary Magdalene comes to resurrection faith. Because verse 11 so naturally follows verse 1, some scholars have speculated that John inserted verses 2–9 into a source that described a single visit by Mary to the tomb. The narrative as it now stands, however, places Mary back at the grave site after running to tell the disciples that it was open. There is nothing implausible in John's sequence of events.

The loss of Jesus' body compounds Mary's mourning and drives her to look into the tomb. Two angels were sitting where Jesus had lain. Their position in the tomb signifies that God, not robbers, touched the body of Jesus. Mary, however, is slow to realize this.

The Johannine and Synoptic accounts of the angelic appearance differ on several points. Matthew and Mark speak of only one angel and all three Synoptics include an angelic announcement of the resurrection (Mt 28:1–6; Mk 16:5–6; Lk 24:1–12). Because Jesus himself is about to appear, John has toned down the impact of the angels considerably. Unlike the Synoptics, he does not mention her fear. The angels ask her a question: "Woman, why are you weeping?"

Mary's response reveals that she still does not understand that God emptied the tomb: "They have taken away my Lord and I do not know where they have laid him." This interchange is virtually repeated after Mary turns around. She sees, but does not recognize, Jesus. He, too, says, "Woman, why are you weeping?" By now, the simple question carries the force of a gentle admonition: there is no reason for weeping, Jesus is standing before her.

Probably because Jesus was buried in a garden, Mary assumes she is speaking with the gardener. Interestingly, several stories developed later in Jewish circles that the gardener had indeed removed the body. If the story was already circulating at the time John wrote, then he counters it in this scene.

More to the point, though, is Mary's failure to recognize her Lord. Jesus has changed. People can no longer relate to him in the same way as they did before his death and resurrection. His physical presence means less and his spiritual presence means more.

When Jesus calls her by name, the truth breaks through her grief. Jesus is alive! She uses her familiar name for him, "Rabbouni," which John translates for his readers as "Teacher" (Jn 20:16). Almost all commentators note how John 10:3 is enacted in this scene: the Good Shepherd calls his sheep by name; they recognize his voice and follow him.

The exchange of names signifies the renewal of their previous relationship. Yet, it is not simply renewed; it is deepened. Evidently, Mary has reached out to Jesus in her joy, for he responds: "Do not hold on to me, because I have not yet ascended to the Father. But go to my brothers and say to them, 'I am ascending to my Father and your Father, to my God and your God' " (Jn 20:17).

Jesus' enigmatic words raise several questions: What does ascension have to do with holding on to Jesus? How do we relate Jesus' caution to Mary with his invitation to Thomas to touch him (Jn 20:27)? When does Jesus ascend to the Father?

No answer can remove all the mystery in these questions. Still, the apparent tension between the experiences of Mary and Thomas lies in the motivation for touching Jesus. The tense of the prohibition in John 20:17 signals that Mary is presently holding on to Jesus and he is asking her to stop. If we take a clue from Matthew 28:9, she is lying in front of Jesus, clutching his feet in adoration. By contrast, Jesus is inviting Thomas to touch his wounds so that Thomas may be convinced of the resurrection.

In other words, Mary must stop clinging to her physical relationship with the earthly Jesus. Thomas must believe that the figure before him stands in continuity with that earthly person. Jesus calls both to move into a deeper spiritual relationship with him, the resurrected Lord.

The ascension of Jesus is more difficult. Consistently, Jesus has taught that his crucifixion marks his "lifting up" and return to the Father. Now he seems to say that he has yet to ascend. A careful reading of verse 17 shows that his ascension is *in process*. John does not draw sharp lines between the crucifixion, resurrection, and ascension.

Jesus' ascension is his return to a pre-existent glorified state that transcends earthly categories of time and space. During the interim period between the resurrection and Jesus' complete return to heavenly glory, his disciples must come to accept this new eternal and spiritual basis for their relationship with Jesus.

To facilitate the transition, Jesus sends Mary to his "brothers" with a message from him: "I am ascending to my Father and your Father, to my God and your God" (Jn 20:17). Jesus uses the language of the new family of God, a family that he inaugurated on the cross (Jn 19:25–27). Mary carries his announcement to the disciples, saying "I have seen the Lord" (Jn 20:18).

The place of Mary Magdalene in the resurrection narratives shows something of John's attitude toward women (see box). A woman was the first to discover the empty tomb, the first to see the risen Lord, and the first to be commissioned to proclaim the good news. In other words, John does not restrict the role of a disciple according to gender.

WOMEN IN THE GOSPEL OF JOHN

The resurrection appearance of Jesus to Mary Magdalene is the last of a number of episodes in which women participate at strategic points in the narrative of Jesus' earthly career.

John 2:1–11, Mary, the Mother of Jesus

Mary, the mother of Jesus, has the faith to approach Jesus when the wedding wine ran out. In response, Jesus foreshadows his "hour," performs his first sign, "revealed his glory; and his disciples believed in him" (Jn 2:11).

John 4:1–42, The Samaritan Woman

Jesus broke the cultural and religious conventions of his time by speaking with a woman in public. More than that, however, he discusses spiritual matters with her. In turn, she becomes a missionary, leading others to faith through her word about Jesus. Jesus' own disciples "reap" where she has "sown."

John 11:20–44, Martha at Lazarus' Resurrection

Martha displays faith and insight as she speaks with Jesus about Lazarus. He tells her, "I am the resurrection and the life" (Jn 11:25). She responds by confessing: ". . . Lord, I believe you are the Messiah, the Son of God, the one coming into the world" (Jn 11:27).

John 12:1–8, Mary, Sister of Martha and Lazarus

While Martha serves (*diakonein*) at table, Mary anoints Jesus with costly perfume in preparation for both his "coronation" and "burial." Jesus defends Mary's action when Judas criticizes it.

John 19:25–27, Mary, the Mother of Jesus, at the Cross

Along with three other women, Jesus' mother follows him to the foot of the cross. All other disciples, except the Beloved Disciple, have abandoned him. By making the Beloved Disciple Mary's son, and she his mother, Jesus not only made provision for his mother's care; he also proclaimed that the crucifixion marks not the end, but the beginning of new relationships in the family of God.

John 20:1–18, Mary Magdalene

Mary Magdalene is the first to discover the empty tomb, the first to see the resurrected Lord, and the first to receive a commission to proclaim the good news of the resurrection. In short, she is first to meet the conditions of apostleship stipulated in other New Testament traditions.

[As well, the incident of the woman caught in adultery (Jn 8:1–11) shows that Jesus did not apply the Mosaic law in a situation where it discriminated against women.]

The Disciples (Jn 20:19–23)

While mourning blinded Mary before Jesus met her, fear crippled the other disciples (Jn 20:19). Afraid of continued persecution from the Jewish authorities, they met behind locked doors. At least one of the twelve, Thomas, was absent (Jn 20:24). John normally does not limit the group of disciples to the twelve, so others may have been present.

Jesus miraculously joins them in the locked room, giving the traditional Jewish greeting "Peace be with you" (Jn 20:19). Physical constraints do not impede his ability to be with his disciples. This illustrates both Jesus' initiative in meeting their need and his bodily transformation.

Jesus' body is not new, it is changed. The wounds on his hands and side show the continuity between the crucified Jesus and the risen Lord. Although John's account of the crucifixion does not mention it, three references here confirm that the soldiers nailed his hands to the cross (Jn 20:20,25,27). The reference to his side recalls the spear thrust (Jn 19:34).

Once the disciples saw the wounds, they realized what it meant and "rejoiced when they saw the Lord" (Jn 20:20). Jesus' earlier promise to them had come true: " . . . you have pain now; but I will see you again, and your hearts will rejoice, and no one will take your joy from you" (Jn 16:22). The resurrected Lord has met them in their fear and given them joyful faith.

Jesus' immediate repetition of the phrase "Peace be with you" (Jn 20:21) elevates the common greeting to a sign that he has conquered the world. He had promised to give them peace that the world could not give them (Jn 14:27; 16:33). Now, victorious through the cross, he can bless believers with the peace of God in all its fullness.

The gift of peace is for mission in the world. Jesus says to his followers, "As the Father has sent me, so I send you" (Jn 20:21). The tenses of the verbs in this commission suggest that the Son's commission continues and believers now share in it. With Christ present in them through the Paraclete, they are empowered to represent God in the world.

After commissioning his disciples, Jesus "breathed on them and said to them 'Receive the Holy Spirit'" (Jn 20:22). The verb translated "breathed" occurs nowhere else in the New Testament. John is probably alluding to Genesis 2:7, where God formed the man and "breathed into his nostrils the breath of life; and the man became a living being." Christ creates new life through his death, resurrection, and bestowal of the Spirit.

Jesus' actions in John 20:22 consummate his earthly ministry. He had come to "baptize with the Holy Spirit" (Jn 1:33). Believers could not receive the Spirit until Jesus was glorified (Jn 7:39). He said he would send the Paraclete after he went away to the Father (Jn 16:7). In view of such foreshadowing, we can only conclude that Jesus has now been glorified. Exalted on the cross, he has ascended to the Father and so can give the promised Spirit.

Interpreters truncate John's complete message when they subordinate it to Luke's Pentecost (Acts 2) by suggesting "John's Pentecost" was an interim measure taken by Christ or that Christ was merely predicting what was to come. Both John and Luke teach that the ascended Christ gave the Spirit to the disciples after he had commissioned them. The date of the event was not the governing factor for either presentation.

Inherent in the disciples' commission is the ongoing work of Christ in the forgiveness and retention of sins (Jn 20:23). During his earthly ministry, Jesus offered forgiveness to anyone who believed in his word. Those who did not believe remained condemned in their sin. Further, Jesus said the Paraclete would "prove the world wrong about sin . . . because they do not believe in me" (Jn 16:8–9).

The disciples are new partners with the Son and the Spirit in their ministry of forgiveness. They are, in effect, pronouncing forgiveness of sins to those who believe and retention of sins for those who reject the Gospel.

Out of this verse, as well as others such as Matthew 16:19 and 18:18, the Roman Catholic Church has developed the sacrament of penance. As well, many interpreters read John 20:23 to refer to admission to baptism. These concerns, however, belong to later periods of church history and should not be projected on the evangelist.

The disciples have seen the risen Lord. Their fear has given way to joy that comes with Christ's peace. They have received both their commission and the Spirit that empowers its fulfillment. It seems that Jesus' earthly ministry has drawn to a close. Yet, there will be another resurrection appearance before the chapter ends.

Thomas (Jn 20:24–29)

Doubt has engulfed Thomas, who was absent from the disciples' previous Sunday gathering. The others have seen the Lord but he insists, "Unless I see the mark of the nails in his hands, and put my finger in the mark of the nails and my hand in his side, I will not believe" (Jn 20:25). Thomas' stance does not represent the voice of

reason over against naiveté. Rather, it typifies faith based on the wondrous character of miracles that Jesus criticizes in John 4:48: "Unless
you see signs and wonders you will not believe."

Twice in the past, Thomas' frank and cynical comments have led
the Gospel reader to deeper spiritual truths (Jn 11:16; 14:5). This
time the question will lead even Thomas to a realization of the truth.
His requirement invokes the grand conclusion of the Gospel of John.

Jesus' third resurrection appearance bears many similarities to
his second: the disciples have repeated Mary's testimony, "We have
seen the Lord" (Jn 20:24, cf. 20:18); they gather on a Sunday behind
locked doors; Jesus suddenly appears in their midst, saying "Peace be
with you"; and, finally, he shows his hands and side.

A stress on belief distinguishes this encounter. Aware of Thomas'
skepticism, Jesus meets his terms. He invites Thomas to touch his
wounds and challenges him with the words "Do not doubt but believe" (Jn 20:27). John's description leads the reader to conclude that
Thomas moves from doubt to faith without actually touching Jesus'
hands and side, for he immediately utters the paramount christological confession of the Gospel: "My Lord and my God!"

As lofty as the title "Lord" is in a creedal context, it is here
overshadowed by the unequivocal use of "God" as a title for Christ.
With this, the Fourth Gospel ends as it began, declaring that Jesus is
God (Jn 1:1). This is both the ultimate and the foundational tenet of
the Christian faith.

It would be easy to overlook the important pronouns in Thomas'
confession. In saying "*my* Lord and *my* God," he is making a personal
profession of belief. John has arranged this entire chapter as a call to
belief for his readers, who have not seen the resurrected Jesus.

While Jesus affirms Thomas' faith based on eye-witness experience, he pronounces a special blessing on "those who have not seen
and yet have come to believe" (Jn 20:29). Like the Beloved Disciple,
who came to resurrection faith without seeing the resurrected Lord,
those who hear the proclaimed word and believe are no less favored
by God. The resurrected Lord meets each individual at his or her
point of insight and kindles faith that transforms adversity into
blessing.

Conclusion (Jn 20:30–31)

Chapter 20 ends with a fitting conclusion to the whole Gospel:

Now Jesus did many other signs in the presence of his disciples, which are not written in this book. But these are writ-

ten so that you may come to believe that Jesus is the Messiah, the Son of God, and that through believing you may have life in his name (Jn 20:30–31).

John's selectivity has a purpose. As discussed in our first chapter, John's statement of purpose probably means that he wrote to deepen the christological understanding in his community more than to issue an evangelistic call to unbelievers. The phrase translated "come to believe" is more accurately translated "continue to believe." Still, an evangelistic thrust fits naturally into John's broader purpose.

In one sense, the Gospel is now complete. However, as it stands, another chapter follows. There were a few unanswered questions and new concerns in the community that gave rise to the epilogue.

STUDY QUESTIONS

1. Compare and contrast the insight of the Beloved Disciple and the rest of disciples that leads to their resurrection faith. In what way is our experience similar to the Beloved Disciple's?

2. What do John's descriptions about Mary Magdalene reveal about the place of women in the church?

3. How would you relate Jesus' caution to Mary not to hold on to him with his invitation to Thomas to touch him?

4. Considering the rest of the Gospel, how would you interpret John 20:22?

5. What are the various interpretations offered for Jesus' words, "If you forgive the sins of any, they are forgiven them; if you retain the sins of any, they are retained" (Jn 20:23)? How would you understand them in the context of the Gospel of John?

6. What does Jesus' question to Thomas and his beatitude in John 20:29 imply? Has Thomas truly believed? Do you think John is saying that the belief of those who have not seen is *better* than that of those disciples who have seen the resurrected Jesus?

7. According to this chapter, can we be sure that Peter has come to resurrection faith? Does he meet the resurrected Lord?

Chapter 16

THE EPILOGUE
(John 21)

Introduction

Even a superficial reading of the last two chapters of John makes one suspect that chapter 21 is an addendum. John 20:30–31 brings the chapter, and the entire Gospel, to a fitting close. Yet, the story continues. We have an additional resurrection appearance, commissioning, and conclusion.

What is more, the lack of unity of the last chapter is apparent. Several scenes that belong to earlier periods of Christ's earthly ministry stand beside references to the deaths of both Peter and the Beloved Disciple. Differences in style, symbolism, and perspective from chapters 1–20 lead to the conclusion that John 21 is an editorial epilogue added after the completion of the original Gospel.

Why did the editor compile this chapter? Clearly there is a concern to preserve some traditions from the Beloved Disciple that were not included in the Gospel (Jn 21:24). However, there were many other traditions that the editor did not preserve (Jn 21:25). Why was this material selected?

A third resurrection appearance to the disciples is important, since it is the only time the Gospel records Peter's presence. Beyond that, the chapter contains important teaching on true discipleship. The commission to evangelize all people is further developed, as is a stress on unity in the church. Notably, Jesus restores Peter after his denials and authorizes his pastoral leadership. Finally, the editor corrects the community's eschatological misunderstanding about the Beloved Disciple.

None of these concerns alone justify chapter 21, but each con-

tributes to a general message for a community facing a crisis of authority. As the Johannine community moved into its second generation, it
was struck by the unexpected death of the Beloved Disciple. The
community was confused and divided.

John 21 helped the Johannine community solidify a relationship
with those churches aligned under Peter's influence. The chapter
authenticates the Beloved Disciple's legacy in the community while
simultaneously commissioning Peter as pastor. The two figures have a
complementary relationship that the editor wished to encourage between the Johannine and Petrine churches.

The supplemental nature of John 21 does not diminish its contribution to the message of the Fourth Gospel. This epilogue is a rich,
highly symbolic chronicle. It effectively brings the Gospel of the Beloved Disciple, and his community, out of its first generation and into
relevance for all succeeding generations of the church.

The Miraculous Catch of Fish (Jn 21:1–14)

Most scholars believe that the narrative of the miraculous catch
of fish and the ensuing breakfast on the shore is a combination of two
stories that originally circulated separately. Luke records two similar
events. According to the Third Gospel, Jesus directed a miraculous
haul of fish in which Peter figured prominently (Lk 5:1–11). Then, at
the first Galilean resurrection appearance, Jesus and his disciples
share a meal of bread and fish (Lk 24:30–31,35,42–43).

The two writers have arranged common traditions differently to
make their points. For the editor of John 21, his agenda included a
resurrection appearance for Peter and the Beloved Disciple.

John 21 opens with Peter announcing a fishing expedition to six
other disciples. The Beloved Disciple was among them (Jn 21:7). The
decision to go fishing does not necessarily mean that the disciples
intend on returning to their old way of life, as some have suggested.
Nevertheless, their work in Christ's absence proves futile; they fish
all night and catch nothing.

As the sun rises, Jesus appears on the beach. Again, the disciples
do not immediately recognize the resurrected Lord. When they follow his direction to cast the net on the starboard side, it fills with fish.

Just as he did with the empty tomb, the Beloved Disciple at once
recognizes the full net as a sign of the resurrection. He tells Peter, "It
is the Lord!" (Jn 21:7; cf. Jn 20:18,25). Peter reacts quickly. The
Greek description is ambiguous, but Peter likely tucked the only gar-

ment he had on, his smock, into his belt. He then plunged into the sea to swim to Jesus.

A few scholars have seen this action as a symbolic foreshadowing of Peter's martyrdom. In John 21:18–19 Jesus says to him, " . . . when you were younger you used to fasten your own belt and go wherever you wished. But when you grow old, you will stretch out your hands, and someone else will fasten a belt around you and take you where you do not wish to go . . . " (Jn 21:18–19).

Once everyone had landed, they found Jesus preparing a meal of fish and bread over a charcoal fire. Before offering the meal to them, he asks Peter to bring some fish from their catch. What happens next is both puzzling and profound:

> . . . Simon Peter went aboard and hauled the net ashore, full of large fish, a hundred and fifty-three of them; and though there were so many, the net was not torn (Jn 21:11).

While on the boat, the entire group of disciples could not haul the net on board (Jn 21:6). Now Peter drags it alone. For some reason, the editor reports that the net contained exactly 153 large fish. Also, he notes that the net remained intact in spite of its heavy load. Compare this to Luke's observation that the nets broke under the strain (Lk 5:6).

Most interpreters agree that symbolism pervades the description. The act of fishing, the role of Peter, and the drawing of the unbroken net are relatively easy to interpret. Elsewhere, fishing has represented the evangelistic mission of disciples (Mt 4:19; Mk 1:17; Lk 5:10). As we shall see later, Peter has come to represent pastoral leadership in the church. The unbroken net conveys unity. The verb used to describe the dragging of the net is the same word used by Jesus in John 12:32: " . . . when I am lifted up from the earth, I will *draw* all people to myself" (cf. also Jn 6:44).

The significance of the 153 fish, however, has baffled commentators for centuries. Many zoological, mathematical, allegorical, and geometrical solutions have been proposed. Generally all interpretations suggest the universality or completeness of the catch. It is best to leave our understanding at that.

Putting all the details of John 21:11 together, we may conclude that the catch of 153 fish in an unbroken net symbolizes the universal character of a unified church. Moreover, the passage singles out Peter. Acting on Jesus' instruction, Peter, and what he symbolizes, will maintain the unity of the church in its mission.

After Peter has fulfilled his task, Jesus offers the disciples break-fast. Initially, Jesus mystifies the disciples, as evidenced by John 21:12: " . . . none of the disciples dared ask him, 'Who are you?' because they knew it was the Lord." Here is another stress on conti-nuity-yet-transformation that marks all the resurrection appearances. The disciples are awe-struck by the risen Lord while still identifying him as the Jesus they know.

In the silence, Jesus takes the initiative. He "came and took the bread and gave it to them, and did the same with the fish" (Jn 21:13). This verse parallels both the content and seaside context of John 6:11, which has eucharistic associations. Consequently, some commenta-tors read this final meal in John eucharistically. Judging by ancient Christian art that illustrated bread and fish at the Lord's supper with seven disciples, early readers of the Gospel also made this connection.

The first section of the epilogue ends with the words, "this was now the third time that Jesus appeared to the disciples after he had been raised from the dead" (Jn 21:14). Following John 20, this is Jesus' third appearance to a *group* of disciples (Jn 20:19,26), al-though he had appeared previously to Mary (Jn 20:14).

The Future of Two Disciples (Jn 21:15–23)

The conversation after breakfast is the most poignant inter-change between Peter and his Lord found in the New Testament. The description ties this scene with Peter's denials of his Lord.

John 21:9 reports a "charcoal fire" (Jn 21:9); the word translated "charcoal fire" also describes the fire over which Peter denied Jesus (John 18:18,25). Since this word occurs only in these two places in the New Testament, John 21 is clearly linked to Peter's denials.

The threefold repetition in both settings also confirms the con-nection. Peter was questioned three times about being a follower of Jesus and he denied it (Jn 18:17,25,27). Now, in John 21:15–17, Jesus asks Peter three times whether Peter loves him.

In each question, Jesus varies his wording. First, Jesus asks, "Si-mon son of John, do you love me more than these?" To the reader, the question is unclear. Jesus could be asking Peter one of three things: "Peter, do you love me more than you love your boat and nets?"; or, "Peter, do you love me more than you love these other disciples?"; or, "Peter, do you love me more than these other disciples love me?"

Whatever was implied in the question, no further comparisons are made. The rest of the narrative concerns only Peter's love for Jesus. Jesus again asks Peter, " . . . do you love me?" (Jn 21:16). For the second time, Peter answers, "Yes, Lord, you know that I love you."

The dialogue contains two different Greek words for love. Jesus uses the word *agapao* and Peter responds with *phileo*. In his third question, however, Jesus uses *phileo* with Peter. Contrary to the speculations of a few scholars, the majority rightly sees simple synonymous stylistic variation here. Such variation is typical of John. At most, we can see a stress on the comprehensiveness of love required of a disciple.

For each confession of Peter's love, Jesus issues a pastoral charge. Peter must now feed and care for the young and the old in the Good Shepherd's flock. In a complete way, Jesus established Peter's pastoral authority over the diverse Christian community.

Jesus and Peter have more unfinished business. In John 13, after Jesus had announced his betrayal and departure to the Father, Peter insisted that he would follow Jesus wherever he went, even to death (Jn 13:37). Jesus corrected him: "You cannot follow me now, but you will follow me afterward" (Jn 13:36).

Now, in chapter 21, Jesus gives Peter the command to follow (Jn 21:19,22). Peter is being called again to become a disciple and assume his pastoral role. More than that, Jesus summons Peter to follow him in death to glorify God (Jn 21:18–19; cf. 12:33).

Later writing reports that Peter was arrested and martyred in Rome under the emperor Nero around A.D. 64 (1 Clement 5:1-6:1). This being the case, the significance of Jesus' words to Peter were unmistakable to the writer of John 21, as he shows in verse 19.

Attention now turns to the Beloved Disciple, who has been quietly "following" Jesus and Peter along the beach. Many interpreters read the reference in a figurative sense. Just as Peter is told to follow Jesus, the Beloved Disciple models what it means to be an ideal disciple: he continues to follow Jesus (Jn 21:20).

With his own destiny laid before him, Peter asks about the Beloved Disciple's future. Perhaps in a spirit of mild rebuke, Jesus says, "If it is my will that he remain until I come, what is that to you? Follow me!" (Jn 21:22). Peter has one role to play in the plan of God, the Beloved Disciple another. It is enough for Peter to be faithful to his calling.

Based on Jesus' words to Peter, some Johannine Christians believed that the Beloved Disciple would live until Christ's second coming (cf. Mt 16:28; Mk 9:1; Lk 9:27). Now the Johannine community faced the unexpected death of the Beloved Disciple. The editor attempts to dispel the apocalyptic misunderstanding.

The explanation offered in John 21:23 may imply that Jesus was speaking to Peter hypothetically. In other words, he is saying even *if* the Beloved Disciple were to live until Christ's second coming, it should be no concern to Peter.

Still, some scholars suggest other interpretations. According to Johannine theology, Jesus returns to his disciples in the Paraclete. If this is how we are to understand the reference to Jesus' coming in John 21:22–23, then the Beloved Disciple has remained until Jesus, in the Spirit, has come again. Yet, this interpretation does not differentiate between Peter and the Beloved Disciple in the same way that Jesus' own words do.

It may be that Jesus' words are truly prophetic. Jesus wants the Beloved Disciple to remain until the eschaton. This does not mean that the disciple will remain physically alive. Instead, he will remain through the distinct legacy he leaves the Johannine community.

If the total message of John 21 is considered, the continuation of the Johannine community is also a concern of the editor. For it to remain, it must be linked to Peter and the churches he represented. Perhaps the anonymity of the Beloved Disciple required the merger with the more secure apostolic traditions as his community entered its second generation.

At least some Johannine Christians eventually followed the lead of the epilogue and entered a partnership with the apostolic stream. The presence of the Johannine literature in the New Testament canon testifies to this development.

Conclusion (Jn 21:24–25)

Scholars who dismiss John 21:24–25 as an exaggerated imitation of the earlier conclusion (Jn 20:30–31) neglect its part in the timeless message of the Fourth Gospel. The epilogue's conclusion confirms the underlying source of the Gospel of John. It ends on a note that recognizes both the grandeur of the Son of God and the limitations of any attempt to testify about him.

Two tenses in John 21:24 reveal the timelessness of the work of the Beloved Disciple. In the past, he has written the accounts from which the editor draws. As a result, in the present, the Beloved Disciple continues to testify about these things. In effect, though he has died, he remains as a true witness to Christ through the community of faith.

His witness has continued to this day. The libraries of the world are still gathering books about the Beloved Disciple's witness to Christ. With each generation that publishes its reflections on his Gospel, John 21:25 seems less an overstatement and more a recognition of the deep mystery of Jesus Christ.

STUDY QUESTIONS

1. What indications are there that chapter 21 is a later addition to the Gospel of John?

2. What does this chapter teach about the nature of true discipleship?

3. How does John 21:11 develop the church's commission to evangelize?

4. Note two indications in John 21 of the risen Jesus' transformed nature.

5. Read John 13:36–38 and 18:15–17. How does John 21:9–19 relate to these earlier passages?

6. Compare the roles of Peter and the Beloved Disciple in this chapter. How do they relate to one another? Is one commended above the other? What relevance might the two figures in relationship have to the Johannine community?

7. Compare Matthew 16:28, Mark 9:1, and Luke 9:27 to John 20:22. How do you interpret the Synoptic sayings? What are three possible ways of interpreting John 20:22?

8. This Gospel has two conclusions. How are they similar? What distinct contribution does each make?

FOR FURTHER READING

The following bibliography is not exhaustive, nor does it contain all the resources used for this book. It does offer, however, a list of recent major works on various aspects of Johannine studies. While many of these are technical works and presuppose a knowledge of Greek, they will be useful for anyone who wishes to delve deeper. For more detailed and specific bibliographical references, consult the two books listed at the end of this bibliography.

Commentaries

Barrett, C. K. *The Gospel According to St. John.* 2d. ed. Philadelphia: The Westminster Press, 1978.

Beasley-Murray, George. *John.* Word Biblical Commentary, no. 36. Waco, Texas: Word, 1987.

Brown, Raymond E. *The Gospel According to John I–XII.* The Anchor Bible, no. 29. Garden City, NY: Doubleday, 1970.

———. *The Gospel According to John XII–XXI.* The Anchor Bible, no. 29A. Garden City, NY: Doubleday, 1970.

Bruce, F. F. *The Gospel of John.* Grand Rapids: Eerdmans, 1983.

Bultmann, Rudolph. *The Gospel of John: A Commentary.* Translated by G. R. Beasley-Murray. Oxford: Basil Blackwell, 1971.

Ellis, Peter F. *The Genius of John: A Composition—Critical Commentary on the Fourth Gospel.* Collegeville, Minnesota: The Liturgical Press, 1984.

Kysar, Robert. *John.* Augsburg Commentary on the New Testament. Minneapolis: Augsburg, 1986.

Lindars, Barnabas. *The Gospel of John.* Grand Rapids: Eerdmans, 1981.

Morris, Leon. *The Gospel According to John.* The New International Commentary on the New Testament. Grand Rapids: Eerdmans, 1971.

Sanders, J. N. and B. A. Mastin. *The Gospel According to St. John.* London: Adam and Charles Black, 1968.

Schnackenburg, Rudolf. *The Gospel According to St. John*, no. 1. New York: Crossroad, 1980.

——. *The Gospel According to St. John*, no. 2. New York: Crossroad, 1981.

——. *The Gospel According to St. John*, no. 3. New York: Crossroad, 1982.

Sloyan, Gerard. *John.* Interpretation, A Bible Commentary for Teaching and Preaching. Atlanta: John Knox Press, 1988.

Chapter 1: A Gospel for All Readers (General Introductions, Background, and Literary Studies):

Borgen, P. *Philo, John, and Paul: New Perspectives on Judaism and Early Christianity.* Brown Judaic Studies, no. 131. Atlanta: Scholars Press, 1987.

Brown, Raymond E. *The Community of the Beloved Disciple.* New York: Paulist Press, 1979.

——. *John and the Dead Sea Scrolls.* Edited by James H. Charlesworth. New York: Harper and Row, 1990.

Brownlee, W. H. *John and Qumran.* Edited by James H. Charlesworth. London: Geoffrey Chapman, 1972.

Buchanan, G. W. "The Samaritan Origin of the Gospel of John." In *Religions in Antiquity*, pp. 149–175. Edited by J. Neusner. Leiden: E. J. Brill, 1968.

Charlesworth, James H. *John and Qumran.* London: Geoffrey Chapman, 1972.

Collins, R. F. *These Things Have Been Written: Studies in the Fourth Gospel.* Grand Rapids: Eerdmans, 1991.

Cullmann, Oscar. *The Johannine Circle.* London: SCM Press, 1976.

Culpepper, R. Alan. *Anatomy of the Fourth Gospel: A Study in Literary Design.* Philadelphia: Fortress, 1983.

——. *The Johannine School.* Missoula: Scholars Press, 1975.

Dodd, C. H. *Historical Tradition in the Fourth Gospel.* New York: Cambridge University Press, 1963.

Duke, Paul D. *Irony in the Fourth Gospel.* Atlanta: John Knox Press, 1985.

Fortna, R. T. *The Fourth Gospel and Its Predecessor: From Narrative Source to Present Gospel*. Philadelphia: Fortress Press, 1988.

——. *The Gospel of Signs*. Cambridge: Cambridge University Press, 1970.

Grundmann, Walter. "The Decision of the Supreme Court to Put Jesus to Death (John 11:47–57) in its Context: Tradition and Redaction in the Gospel of John." In *Jesus and the Politics of His Day*. Edited by C. F. D. Bammel. New York: Cambridge University Press, 1984.

Martyn, J. Louis. *History and Theology in the Fourth Gospel*. Nashville: Abingdon, 1979.

Painter, John. "Christology and the History of the Johannine Community in the Prologue of the Fourth Gospel." *New Testament Studies* 30 (1984):460–474.

——. "The Farewell Discourses and the History of Johannine Christianity." *New Testament Studies* 27 (1981):526, 528, 530–534.

——. *John. Witness and Theologian*. 2d. ed. London: SPCK, 1979.

Pancaro, Severino. *The Law in the Fourth Gospel: The Torah and the Gospel, Moses and Jesus, Judaism and Christianity According to John*. Leiden: E. J. Brill, 1975.

Reim, Gunther. "Jesus as God in the Fourth Gospel; the Old Testament Background." *New Testament Studies* 30 (1984):158–160.

Smalley, Stephen S. *John: Evangelist and Interpreter*. Exeter: Paternoster Press, 1978.

Smith, Dwight Moody Jr. *The Composition and Order of the Fourth Gospel: Bultmann's Literary Theory*. Yale Publications in Religion, no. 10. New Haven: Yale University Press, 1965.

——. *Johannine Christianity*. Columbia, South Carolina: University of South Carolina Press, 1986.

Von Wahlde, Urban C. *The Earliest Version of John's Gospel: Recovering the Gospel of Signs*. Wilmington: Michael Glazier, 1989.

Whitacre, Rodney. *Johannine Polemic: The Role of Tradition and Theology*. Missoula: Scholars Press, 1982.

Woll, Bruce D. *Johannine Christianity in Conflict: Authority, Rank and Succession in the First Farewell Discourse*. Chico, CA: Scholars Press, 1981.

Chapter 2: Jesus Christ: God in the Flesh (John 1)

Borgen, P. "The Logos Was the True Light. Contributions to the Interpretation of the Prologue of John." *Novum Testamentum* 14 (1972): 115–130.

Culpepper, R. Alan. "The Pivot of John's Prologue." *New Testament Studies* 27 (1981):1–31.

Miller, E. L. *Salvation-History in the Prologue of John. The Significance of John 1:3–4.* Supplements to Novum Testamentum, no. 60. New York: E. J. Brill, 1989.

Painter, John. "Christology and the History of the Johannine Community in the Prologue of the Fourth Gospel." *New Testament Studies* 30 (1984):460–474.

Chapter 3: New Beginnings: For the Jews (John 2–3)

Nicol, W. *The Semeia in the Fourth Gospel.* Leiden: E. J. Brill, 1972.

Olsson, Birger. *Structure and Meaning in the Fourth Gospel: A Text-Linguistic Analysis of John 2:1–11 and 4:1–42.* Lund: Gleerup, 1974.

Chapter 4: New Beginnings: For the World (John 4)

Boers, Hendrikus. *Neither on This Mountain nor in Jerusalem: A Study of John 4.* Atlanta: Scholars Press, 1988.

Okure, Teresa. *The Johannine Approach to Mission: A Contextual Study of John 4:1–42.* Tübingen: J.C.B. Mohr, 1988.

Olsson, Birger. *Structure and Meaning in the Fourth Gospel: A Text-Linguistic Analysis of John 2:1–11 and 4:1–42.* Lund: Gleerup, 1974.

Chapter 5: Doing the Work of God: The Lord of the Sabbath (John 5)

Davies, W. D. *The Gospel and the Land.* Berkeley: University of California Press, 1974.

Meeks, Wayne A. *The Prophet-King, Moses Traditions and the Johannine Christology.* Leiden: E. J. Brill, 1967. PG

Pancaro, Severino. *The Law in the Fourth Gospel: The Torah and the Gospel, Moses and Jesus, Judaism and Christianity According to John.* Leiden: E. J. Brill, 1975.

Temple, Sydney. *The Core of the Fourth Gospel.* London: Mowbrays, 1975.

Trites, A. A. *The New Testament Concept of Witness.* Cambridge: Cambridge University Press, 1977.

Von Wahlde, Urban C. "The Witness to Jesus in John 5:31–40 and Belief in the Fourth Gospel." *Catholic Biblical Quarterly* 43 (1981):385–404.

Chapter 6: Doing the Work of God: The Bread of Life (John 6)

Borgen, P. *Bread from Heaven: An Exegetical Study in the Concept of the Manna in the Gospel of John and the Writing of Philo.* Leiden: E. J. Brill, 1965.
Harner, Philip B. *The 'I Am' of the Fourth Gospel: A Study in Johannine Usage and Thought.* Philadelphia: Fortress, 1970.

Chapter 7: Confrontations: The Provocative Teacher (John 7)

Davies, W. D. *The Gospel and the Land.* Berkeley: University of California Press, 1974.
Meeks, Wayne A. *The Prophet-King, Moses Traditions and the Johannine Christology.* Leiden: E. J. Brill, 1972.
Pancaro, Severino. *The Law in the Fourth Gospel: The Torah and the Gospel, Moses and Jesus, Judaism and Christianity According to John.* Leiden: E. J. Brill, 1975.
Temple, Sydney. *The Core of the Fourth Gospel.* London: Mowbrays, 1975.

Chapter 8: Confrontations: The Revealing Light (John 8–9)

Burge, Gary. "A Specific Problem in the New Testament Text and Canon: The Woman Caught in Adultery (John 7:53–8:11)." *Journal of the Evangelical Theological Society* 27 (1984): 141–148.
Lindars, Barnabas. "Slave and Son in John 8:31–36." In *The New Testament Age: Essays in Honor of Bo Reicke,* pp. 271–286. Edited by William C. Weinrich. Macon, GA: Mercer University Press, 1984.
Riga, Peter J. "The Man Born Blind." *The Bible Today* 22 (1984): 158–160.

Chapter 9: Laying Down His Life: Final Foreshadowing (John 10–11)

Beutler, Johannes and Robert Fortna, eds. *The Shepherd Discourse of John 10 and its Context.* New York: Cambridge University Press, 1990.

Grundmann, Walter. "The Decision of the Supreme Court to Put Jesus to Death (John 11:47–57) in its Context: Tradition and Redaction in the Gospel of John." In *Jesus and the Politics of His Day*. Edited by C. F. D. Bammel. New York: Cambridge University Press, 1984.

Chapter 10: Laying Down His Life: Leaving the Public Eye (John 12)

Meeks, Wayne A. *The Prophet-King, Moses Traditions and the Johannine Christology*. Leiden: E. J. Brill, 1972.
Temple, Sydney. *The Core of the Fourth Gospel*. London: Mowbrays, 1975.
Trites, A. A. *The New Testament Concept of Witness*. Cambridge: Cambridge University Press, 1977.

Chapter 11: Parting Words to the Faithful: Preparations for Departure (John 13)

Kurz, William S. *Farewell Addresses in the New Testament*. Collegeville, MN: Liturgical Press, 1990.
Quast, Kevin. *Peter and the Beloved Disciple: Figures for a Community in Crisis*. Journal for the Study of the New Testament Supplement Series, no. 32. Sheffield: Sheffield Academic Press, 1989.
Segovia, Fernando F. *Love Relationships in the Johannine Tradition: agape/agapan in 1 John and the Fourth Gospel*. Missoula: Scholars Press, 1982.
Woll, Bruce D. *Johannine Christianity in Conflict: Authority, Rank and Succession in the First Farewell Discourse*. Chico, CA: Scholars Press, 1981.

Chapter 12: Parting Words to the Faithful: Promises for the Future (John 14–16)

Burge, Gary. *The Anointed Community: The Holy Spirit in the Johannine Tradition*. Grand Rapids: Eerdmans, 1987.
Casurella, Anthony. *The Johannine Paraclete in the Church Fathers: A Study in the History of Exegesis*. Tübingen: JCB Mohr, 1983.
Franck, Eskil. *Revelation Taught: The Paraclete in the Gospel of John*. Lund: Gleerup, 1985.

Kurz, William S. *Farewell Addresses in the New Testament.* College-ville, MN: Liturgical Press, 1990.

Lussier, Ernest. *Christ's Farewell Discourse.* New York: Alba House, 1979.

Segovia, Fernando F. *Love Relationships in the Johannine Tradition: agape/agapan in 1 John and the Fourth Gospel.* Missoula: Scholars Press, 1982.

Chapter 13: The Hour of Glorification: Alone on Behalf of Others (John 17)

Appold, Mark L. *The Oneness Motif in the Fourth Gospel.* Tübingen: J. C. B. Mohr, 1976.

Käsemann, Ernst. *The Testament of Jesus.* London: SCM Press, 1968.

Kurz, William S. *Farewell Addresses in the New Testament.* College-ville, MN: Liturgical Press, 1990.

Chapter 14: The Hour of Glorification: Crucifixion and Exaltation (John 18–19)

Benoit, P. *The Passion and Resurrection of Jesus Christ.* New York: Herder and Herder, 1969.

Bligh, John. *The Sign of the Cross. The Passion and Resurrection of Jesus According to St. John.* Slough: St. Paul Publications, 1975.

Fenton, J. C. *The Passion According to John.* London: SPCK, 1961.

Potterie, I. de la. *The Hour of Jesus. The Passion and the Resurrection of Jesus According to John: Text and Spirit.* Translated by G. Murray. Middlegreen, Slough: St. Paul Publications, 1989.

Chapter 15: The Resurrection Appearances: "That You May Believe"(John 20)

Benoit, P. *The Passion and Resurrection of Jesus Christ.* New York: Herder and Herder, 1969.

Bligh, John. *The Sign of the Cross. The Passion and Resurrection of Jesus According to St. John.* Slough: St. Paul Publications, 1975.

Bode, Edward Lynn. *The First Easter Morning.* Rome: Biblical Institute Press, 1970.

Potterie, I. de la. *The Hour of Jesus. The Passion and the Resurrection of Jesus According to John: Text and Spirit.* Translated by G. Murray. Middlegreen, Slough, UK: St Paul Publications, 1989.

Quast, Kevin. *Peter and the Beloved Disciple: Figures for a Community in Crisis.* Journal for the Study of the New Testament Supplement Series, no. 32. Sheffield: Sheffield Academic Press, 1989.

Chapter 16: The Epilogue (John 21)

McHugh, J. "The Original Functions of John 21." *Journal of Biblical Literature* 102 (1983):85–98.

Osborne, Grant R. "John 21: A Test Case for History and Redaction in the Resurrection Narratives." In *Gospel Perspectives II.* Edited by R. T. France and D. Wenham. Sheffield: Sheffield Academic Press, 1982.

Quast, Kevin. *Peter and the Beloved Disciple: Figures for a Community in Crisis.* Journal for the Study of the New Testament Supplement Series, no. 32. Sheffield: Sheffield Academic Press, 1989.

Shaw, Alan. "Image and Symbol in John 21." *Expository Times* 86 (1975):311.

Smalley, Stephen S. "The Sign in John xxi." *New Testament Studies* 20 (1964):273–288.

Johannine Theology

Ashton, John. *Understanding the Fourth Gospel.* Oxford: Oxford University Press, 1991.

Dodd, C. H. *The Interpretation of the Fourth Gospel.* Cambridge: Cambridge University Press, 1953.

Forestell, J. Terence. *The Word of the Cross: Salvation as Revelation in the Fourth Gospel.* Rome: Biblical Institute Press, 1974.

Gruenler, Royce Gordon. *The Trinity in the Gospel of John: A Thematic Commentary on the Fourth Gospel.* Grand Rapids: Baker Book House, 1986.

Harner, Philip B. *The 'I Am' of the Fourth Gospel: A Study in Johannine Usage and Thought.* Philadelphia: Fortress, 1970.

Lindars, Barnabas. "The Son of Man in Johannine Christology." In *Christ and Spirit in the New Testament: Studies in Honour of C. F. D. Moule.* Edited by Barnabas Lindars and Stephen Smalley. Cambridge: Cambridge University Press, 1973.

Loader, William R. G. *Christology of the Fourth Gospel: Structure and Issues.* Frankfurt: Peter Lang, 1989.

Morris, Leon. *Jesus is the Christ: Studies in the Theology of John*. Grand Rapids: Eerdmans, 1989.

Nicholson, Godfrey. *Death as Departure: The Johannine Descent-Ascent Schema*. SBL Dissertation Series, no. 63. Chico, CA: Scholars Press, 1983.

O'Day, Gail. *Revelation in the Fourth Gospel: Narrative Mode and Theological Claim*. Philadelphia: Fortress Press, 1986.

O'Grady, John F. "The Human Jesus in the Fourth Gospel." *Biblical Theology Bulletin* 14 (1984):63–66.

Pollard, T. E. *Johannine Christology and the Early Church*. Cambridge: Cambridge University Press, 1970.

Reim, Gunther. "Jesus as God in the Fourth Gospel; the Old Testament Background." *New Testament Studies* 30 (1984):158–160.

Smalley, Stephen S. *John: Evangelist and Interpreter*. Exeter: Paternoster Press, 1978.

Smith, Dwight Moody Jr. *Johannine Christianity*. Columbia, South Carolina: University of South Carolina Press, 1986.

Thompson, Marianne Meye. *The Humanity of Jesus in the Fourth Gospel*. Philadelphia: Fortress, 1988.

Bibliography

Van Belle, G. *Johannine Bibliography 1966–1985. A Cumulative Bibliography on the Fourth Gospel*. Bibliotheca Ephemeridum Theologicarum Lovaniensium, no. 82. Leuven: Leuven University Press, 1988.

Wagner, Gunther, ed. *An Exegetical Bibliography of the New Testament: John and 1, 2, 3 John*. Macon, GA: Mercer University Press, 1987.

SUBJECT INDEX

abiding in Jesus 45, 55, 102, 104
Abraham 68, 70, 71, 76, 92, 93
abundant life 3, 35, 39, 50, 80, 82, 104
adultery 6, 69, 135
advocate, the Holy Spirit as 102, 105–107
agapao 144
alabaster 88
allegories 78, 142
ambiguities 1, 17, 24, 33
Andrew 14, 49, 52, 89
Annas 122
"Anointed" (Messiah) 15, 16, 125
anointing of Jesus 82, 88, 93
anonymity 2, 14, 145
Antichrist 115
apocalyptic eschatology 4, 15, 17, 64, 91, 145
apostasy 107
apostleship 135
Aramaic 41, 125
ascension 17, 26, 56, 62, 91, 128, 133–134
atonement 15, 24
attorney, Holy Spirit as 105
Augustine 132

authorities (see religious authorities)
authority
  of Jesus 41–43, 47, 57, 59, 62, 63, 68, 81
  of the Spirit 5
authorship of the Gospel 4, 6, 8

bandits (see thieves)
baptism 25, 26, 28, 29, 33, 74, 95, 127, 137
bath (see footwashing)
believers 2, 33, 43, 47, 55, 62, 70, 82, 92, 95, 101, 105, 108, 109, 111–114, 117, 119, 122, 127, 136, 137
believing 4, 5, 7, 8, 10, 14, 17, 26, 27, 37, 38, 44–46, 54–57, 59, 61, 63, 68, 70, 73–77, 82, 84, 92, 96, 99, 103, 106, 112, 113, 115–118, 129, 130, 132, 134, 137–139, 141
Beloved Disciple 2, 4–6, 10, 14, 83, 88, 97, 99, 123, 126, 127, 128–132, 135, 138–141, 144–146
belt, Peter's 142

156

sword 120
symbolism 1, 2, 15, 22, 24, 25,
    27, 35, 49, 72, 89, 119,
    126, 128, 131, 140–142
synagogue 27, 75, 77, 92, 107,
    122
Synoptics 6, 49, 78, 87, 90, 93,
    100, 125, 133, 146

tabernacle 14
targums 64
temple 22–24, 28, 59–63, 71,
    76, 89, 104, 119, 120, 122
tent 13, 14
testimony 4, 14, 15, 27, 37, 44,
    45, 47, 52, 61, 69, 70, 72,
    75, 95, 103, 106, 107, 138,
    145
"the Jews" 19, 24, 28, 32, 33,
    36, 39, 43–46, 50, 62, 66,
    70, 71, 75, 77, 82, 85, 98,
    119, 122–128
thieves 79, 80, 86
thirst 32–34, 36, 38, 65, 126
Thomas 83, 84, 102, 103, 129,
    130, 134, 136–139
three 2, 5, 19, 22, 24, 40, 48,
    56, 58, 60, 67, 70, 77, 78,
    82, 84, 87, 92, 98, 101,
    110–112, 120, 122, 123,
    128, 133, 135, 136, 142,
    143, 146
throne 12, 91, 92, 127
tomb 84, 85, 127, 129–135, 141
Torah 11, 32–34, 45, 69
torches 60, 68, 72, 76, 120
transformation of Jesus'
    resurrected body 136, 143
Trinity 2, 3, 13, 108
truth 1–3, 13, 17, 20, 32, 35,
    39, 43, 45, 54, 64, 68, 70,
    71, 83, 92, 101–103, 105–

109, 113, 115, 116, 118,
    123, 125, 133, 138
twelve 25, 50, 56, 83, 101, 113,
    136

unbelief 57, 59, 66, 76, 91–93,
    108
unbelievers 2, 46, 55, 56, 70,
    139
unity 3, 13, 32, 36, 39, 43, 47,
    49, 57, 81, 96, 101, 103,
    111, 112, 113, 116–118,
    126, 132, 140, 142
universalism 72, 89, 142

vine 54, 101, 102, 104, 109
vinedresser 104
vinegar 126
vineyard 101, 104

water 2, 12, 19–22, 25, 26, 28–
    30, 32–37, 39, 42, 47, 48,
    52, 60, 61, 65–68, 95, 127
waterpots 2, 20, 22
wedding 19, 20, 27, 135
weeping 133
wheat 89
wilderness 21, 48, 49, 57, 60, 61
wind (see also *pneuma*) 25
wine 2, 19–22, 28, 55, 60, 126,
    135
wisdom 1, 4, 11, 12, 34, 55, 105
witness 5, 27, 44, 45, 47, 68,
    69, 89, 105, 108, 109, 112,
    116, 117, 122, 129, 132,
    138, 145, 146
wolves 80
women 6, 21, 29, 30, 32, 33,
    35–37, 39, 60, 61, 69, 72,
    83, 84, 87, 122, 126, 129,
    131, 133, 134, 135, 139